Augsburg's Drawing

BOOK II.

A Text Book of Drawing Designed for Use in the Fourth, Fifth, Sixth, Seventh and Eighth Grades

BY

D. R. Augsburg

Director of Drawing in the Public Schools of Oakland, Cal.

Copyright © 2013 Read Books Ltd.
This book is copyright and may not be
reproduced or copied in any way without
the express permission of the publisher in writing

British Library Cataloguing-in-Publication Data
A catalogue record for this book is available from the
British Library

Drawing and Illustration

Drawing is a form of visual art that can make use of any number of drawing instruments, including graphite pencils, pen and ink, inked brushes, wax colour pencils, crayons, charcoal, chalk, pastels and various kinds of erasers, markers, styluses, metals (such as silverpoint) and even electronic drawing. As a medium, it has been one of the most popular and fundamental means of public expression throughout human history – as one of the simplest and most efficient means of communicating visual ideas.

Drawing itself long predates other forms of human communication, with evidence for its existence preceding that of the written word – demonstrated in cave paintings of around 40,000 years ago. These drawings, known as pictograms, depicted objects and abstract concepts including animals, human hands and generalised patterns. Over time, these sketches and paintings were stylised and simplified, leading to the development of the written language as we know it today. This form of drawing can truly be considered art in its purest sense – the basic forms on which all others build.

Whilst the term 'to draw' derives from the Old English *dragan* (meaning 'to drag, draw or protract'), the word 'illustrate' derives from the Latin word *illustratio*, meaning 'enlighten' or 'irradiate'. This process of 'enlightenment' is central to drawing and illustration as we know it today. Medieval codices' illustrations were often called 'illuminations', designed to highlight and further explain important aspects of biblical texts. This was the most general form of illustration; hand-created, individual and unique. This changed in the fifteenth century however, when books began to be illustrated with woodcuts – most notably in Germany, by Albrecht Dürer.

The first creative impulses of a painter or sculptor are commonly expressed in drawings, and architects and photographers are commonly trained to draw, if for no other reason than to train their perceptual skills and develop their creative potential. Initially, artists used and re-used wooden tablets for the production of their drawings, however following the widespread availability of paper in the fourteenth century, the use of drawing in the arts increased. During the Renaissance (a period of massive flourishing of human intellectual endeavours and creativity), drawings exhibiting realistic and representational qualities emerged. Notable draftsmen included Leonardo da Vinci, Michelangelo and Raphael. They were inspired by the concurrent developments in geometry and philosophy, exhibiting a true synthesis of these branches – a combination somewhat lost in the modern day.

Figure drawing became a recognised subsection of artistic drawing in this period, despite its long history stretching back to prehistoric descriptions. An anecdote by the Roman author and philosopher Pliny, describes how Zeuxis (a painter who flourished during the 5th century BCE) reviewed the young women of Agrigentum naked before selecting five whose features he would combine in order to paint an ideal image. The use of nude models in the medieval artist's workshop is further implied in the writings of Cennino Cennini (an Italian painter), and a manuscript of Villard de Honnecourt confirms that sketching from life was an established practice by the thirteenth century. The Carracci, who opened their *Accademia degli Incamminati* (one of the first art academies in Italy) in Bologna in the 1580s, set the pattern for later art schools by making life drawing the central discipline. The course of training began with the copying of engravings, then proceeded to drawing from plaster casts, after which the students were trained in drawing from the live model.

The main processes for reproduction of drawings and illustrations in the sixteenth and seventeenth centuries were engraving and etching, and by the end of the eighteenth century, lithography (a method of printing originally based on the immiscibility of oil and water) allowed even better illustrations to be reproduced. In the later seventeenth and eighteenth centuries, the previous combination of the arts and sciences in drawing gave way to a more romantic and even classical style, epitomised by draftsmen such as Poussin, Rembrandt, Rubens, Tiepolo and Antoine Watteau. Mastery in drawing was considered a prerequisite to painting, and students in Jacques-Louis David's Studio (a famed eighteenth century French painter of the neo-classical style), were required to draw for six hours a day, from a model who remained in the same pose for an entire week!

During this period, an increasingly large gap started to emerge between 'fine artists' on the one hand, and 'draftsmen' / 'illustrators' on the other. This difference became further complicated with the 'Golden Age of Illustration'; a period customarily defined as lasting from the latter quarter of the nineteenth century until just after the First World War. In this period of no more than fifty years the popularity, abundance and most importantly the unprecedented upsurge in quality of illustrated works marked an astounding change in the way that publishers, artists and the general public came to view artistic drawing. Arthur Rackham, Walter Crane, John Tenniel and William Blake are some of its most famous names. Until the latter part of the nineteenth century, the work of illustrators was largely proffered anonymously, and in England it was only after Thomas Bewick's pioneering technical advances in wood engraving that it became common to acknowledge the artistic and technical expertise of illustrators. Such draftsmen also frequently used their drawings in preparation for paintings, further obfuscating the distinction between drawing/painting, high/low art.

The artists involved in the Arts and Crafts Movement (with a strong emphasis on stylised drawing, and a powerful influence on the 'Golden Age of Illustration') also attempted to counter the ever intruding Industrial Revolution, by bringing the values of beautiful and inventive craftsmanship back into the sphere of everyday life. This helped to counter the main challenge which emerged around this time – photography. The invention of the first widely available form of photography (with flexible photographic film role marketed in 1885) led to a shift in the use of drawing in the arts. This new technology took over from drawing as a superior method of accurately representing the visual world, and many artists abandoned their painstaking drawing practices. As a result of these developments however, modernism in the arts emerged – encouraging 'imaginative originality' in drawing and abstract formulations. Drawing was once again at the forefront of the arts.

There are many different categories of drawing, including figure drawing, cartooning, doodling and shading. There are also many drawing methods, such as line drawing, stippling, shading, hatching, crosshatching, creating textures and tracing – and the artist must be aware of complex problems such as form, proportion and perspective (portrayed in either linear methods, or depth through tone and texture). Today, there are also many computer-aided drawing tools, which are utilised in design, architecture, engineering, as well as the fine arts. It is often exploratory, with considerable emphasis on observation, problem-solving and composition, and as such, remains an unceasingly useful tool in the artists repertoire.

The processes of drawing is a fascinating artistic practice, enabling a beautiful array of effects and creative expression. As is evident from this short introduction, it also has an incredibly old history, moving from decorations on cave walls to the most advanced, realistic and imaginative drawings possible in the present day. It is hoped that the current reader enjoys this book on the subject.

PREFACE.

Augsburg's Drawing System is embraced in three books, and is designed for use in graded and ungraded schools. Each subject is treated topically and is arranged so as to give the widest latitude and the greatest flexibility in teaching.

Book I. is a teacher's hand book, showing simple and effective methods of teaching drawing, including color work, in the first, second and third grades.

Book II. is a regular text book, containing the essentials of Free Hand Drawing. It may be placed in the hands of the pupils of the fourth, fifth, sixth, seventh and eighth grades, and used the same as a text book in arithmetic or other subjects. It may also be used in connection with a system of copy or blank books or drawing pads.

Book III. contains short, yet complete, courses in Brush Drawing, Wash Drawing, Water Color Drawing, Pen Drawing, the drawing of the Human Head and Figure, Decorative Design and Constructive Drawing.

CONTENTS.

	PAGE
GENERAL OUTLINE	7
CHAPTER I.	
THE PERSPECTIVE PRINCIPLE	15
CHAPTER II.	
THE BOX AS A TYPE FORM	32
CHAPTER III.	
THE CUBE AS A TYPE FORM	44
CHAPTER IV.	
APPLICATION OF THE BOX FORM	56
CHAPTER V.	
OBLIQUE DRAWING	73
CHAPTER VI.	
EXACT DRAWING	83
CHAPTER VII.	
THE CYLINDER AS A TYPE FORM	92
CHAPTER VIII.	
APPLICATION OF THE CYLINDER	108
CHAPTER IX.	
OBJECT DRAWING	117
CHAPTER X.	
THE TRIANGULAR PRISM AS A TYPE FORM	141
CHAPTER XI.	
REFLECTIONS	152

INTRODUCTION.

GENERAL OUTLINE.

Books II. and III. form a complete text-book in Drawing, Color, Designing and Constructive Drawing and therefore contain more than can be compassed in an ordinary school course in drawing. To meet the varying demands in this subject, and to make the books of the widest utility, the following courses have been outlined:

The Standard Course.
The Pictorial Course.
The Designing Course.
The Constructive Drawing Course.
The Ungraded Course.
The Teacher's Course.
The High School Course.

The Standard Course is both general and fundamental in character, and aims to aid in preparing the pupil for whatever calling he may follow in life: to make him a better blacksmith, carpenter, machinist, miner, farmer; to make her a better dressmaker, milliner, housekeeper, teacher; to prepare both for all of life's duties in which skill of hand and mind are factors.

The Pictorial Course is the same as the standard course, with the addition of pen drawing and the study of the human head and figure in the seventh and eighth grades.

The Designing Course contains a course in designing in the sixth, seventh and eighth grades; otherwise it is similar to the standard course.

The Constructive Drawing Course contains a course in Constructive or Mechanical drawing in the sixth, seventh and eighth grades; otherwise it, also, is like the standard course.

The Ungraded Course is a course in drawing for ungraded schools. It is arranged for one class containing two divisions: one composed of first, second and third year pupils, and the other of fourth, fifth, sixth, seventh and eighth year pupils.

The High School Course is entirely in Book III. The course is a continuation of the work of the grades in Brush and Wash drawing, Water Colors, Pen drawing, Designing and Constructive drawing.

These courses are not intended to be arbitrary in character, but suggestive. They are intended to outline, in a general way, what can be taught to advantage in each grade.

The Mediums used in this system are those used most frequently in the trades and professions, *viz.: the lead pencil, water colors, ink and the blackboard crayon.*

Lead Pencils.— A soft lead pencil capable of the widest range of line should be used, one capable of making light, medium and black lines.

Water Colors.— The mechanical use of water colors should be taught in the second and third grades and then used in all grades above the third as a common medium in all work in which color can be used to advantage.

Ink is used in pen and brush drawing and may be used in place of the pencil in other lines of work.

Crayon is the most common medium used by the teacher in giving instruction. The blackboard has no superior.

Ambidextrous or Two-Handed Drawing may be used in each grade as an exercise to gain freedom, speed and skill in the use of the hands. The exercises should not be more than five minutes long. Ambidextrous exercises may be found in Book I.; also in Book III. under the head of *Designing by Form*.

Action Drawing. It is well to take up the study of a bird and an animal in each grade. In Book I., under the head of *The Drawing of Birds* and *The Drawing of Animals*, this work is shown in detail.

Object Drawing is given a prominent place in every grade from the first to the eighth. In all of the courses much time should be given to object drawing. Pupils should be taught to seek the object as a source and perfecting element of the mental image. Object drawing should be introduced at pleasure through the year's work.

The courses in detail are as follows:

THE STANDARD COURSE.

Length of drawing period should be fifteen minutes per day. This should give at least ten minutes of actual drawing.

GRADE IV.
- Chapter 1. The perspective principle.
- Chapter 2. The box as a type form.
- Chapter 3. The cube as a type form.
- Chapter 4. Application of the box form.
- Chapter 9. Object drawing.

GRADE V.
- Chapter 5. Oblique drawing.
- Chapter 6. Exact drawing.
- Chapter 7. The cylinder as a type form.
- Chapter 9. Object drawing.

GRADE VI.
- Chapter 8. Application of the cylinder.
- Chapter 9. Object drawing.
- Chapter 10. The triangular prism as a type form.
- Chapter 1. Book III. Brush drawing.

GRADE VII.
- Chapter 11. Reflections.
- Chapter 2. Book III. Wash drawing.
- Chapter 9. Object drawing.

GRADE VIII.
- Chapter 3. Book III. Water colors.
- Chapter 9. Object drawing.

PICTORIAL COURSE.

Length of drawing period should be fifteen minutes per day.

GRADE IV.
- Chapter 1. The perspective principle.
- Chapter 2. The box as a type form.
- Chapter 3. The cube as a type form.
- Chapter 4. The application of the box form.
- Chapter 9. Object drawing.

GRADE V.
- Chapter 5. Oblique drawing.
- Chapter 6. Exact drawing.
- Chapter 7. The cylinder as a type form.
- Chapter 9. Object drawing.

GRADE VI.
- Chapter 8. Application of the cylinder.
- Chapter 9. Object drawing.
- Chapter 10. The triangular prism as a type form.
- Chapter 1. Book III. Brush drawing.

GRADE VII.
- Chapter 11. Reflections.
- Chapter 2. Book III. Wash drawing.
- Chapter 4. Book III. Pen drawing.
- Chapter 9. Object drawing.

GRADE VIII.
- Chapter 3. Book III. Water colors.
- Chapter 5. Book III. The human head and figure.
- Chapter 9. Object drawing.

DESIGNING COURSE.

The length of drawing period should be fifteen minutes each day.

GRADE IV.
> Chapter 1. The perspective principle.
> Chapter 2. The box as a type form.
> Chapter 3. The cube as a type form.
> Chapter 4. Application of the box form.
> Chapter 9. Object drawing.

GRADE V.
> Chapter 5. Oblique drawing.
> Chapter 6. Exact drawing.
> Chapter 7. The cylinder as a type form.
> Chapter 9. Object drawing.

GRADE VI.
> Chapter 8. Application of the cylinder.
> Chapter 9. Object drawing.
> Chapter 10. The triangular prism as a type form.
> Chapter 6. Book III. Designing by line.

GRADE VII.
> Chapter 11. Reflections.
> Chapter 7. Book III. Designing by form.
> Chapter 9. Object drawing.

GRADE VIII.
> Chapter 9. Object drawing.
> Chapter 3. Book III. Water colors.
> Chapter 8. Book III. Foliation.

CONSTRUCTIVE DRAWING COURSE.

The length of the drawing period should be fifteen minutes each day.

GRADE IV.
- Chapter 1. The perspective principle.
- Chapter 2. The box as a type form.
- Chapter 3. The cube as a type form.
- Chapter 4. Application of the box form.
- Chapter 9. Object drawing.

GRADE V.
- Chapter 5. Oblique drawing.
- Chapter 6. Exact drawing.
- Chapter 7. The cylinder as a type form.
- Chapter 9. Object drawing.

GRADE VI.
- Chapter 8. Application of the cylinder.
- Chapter 9. Object drawing.
- Chapter 10. The triangular prism as a type form.
- Chapter 9. Book III. Constructive drawing.

GRADE VII.
- Chapter 11. Reflections.
- Chapter 9. Object drawing.
- Chapter 10. Book III. Isometric and Cabinet drawing.

GRADE VIII.
- Chapter 9. Object drawing.
- Chapter 3. Book III. Water colors.
- Chapter 11. Book III. Orthographic projection.

THE UNGRADED COURSE.

The length of the drawing lesson should be fifteen minutes per day.

Divide the school into two divisions as follows:

DIVISION 1. First, second and third year pupils.
DIVISION 2. Fourth, fifth, sixth, seventh and eighth year pupils.

Both divisions may draw during the same period, but the teaching should alternate from one to the other.

Some subjects may be taught to both divisions in common. For example, in *Object Drawing*, the first division may draw a single leaf, the second division a spray of leaves.

The following subjects may be taught in both divisions at the same time:

Object drawing.
Memory and imaginative drawing.
Two-handed drawing.
Action drawing.
Birds and Animals.
Brush drawing.
Water colors. Book I.

The following subjects should be taught separately, alternating from one division to the other in teaching:

DIVISION 1. Book I.
    Chapter 5. Place and relation of objects.
    Chapter 6. The relative size of objects.
    Chapter 7. Proportion.
    Chapter 8. Unity.

DIVISION 2. Book II.
   Chapter 1. The perspective principle.
   Chapter 2. The box as a type form.
   Chapter 3. The cube as a type form.
   Chapter 4. Application of the box form.
   Chapter 5. Oblique drawing.
   Chapter 6. Exact drawing.
   Chapter 7. The cylinder as a type form.
   Chapter 8. Application of the cylinder.

Encourage individual work among the larger pupils. This can be done if each has a text-book of his own, so that individual work can be done the same as in arithmetic.

TEACHERS' COURSE.

Book II. forms a teachers' course by beginning with Chapter 1 and following the order given.

HIGH SCHOOL COURSE.

   Chapter 1. Book III. Brush drawing.
   Chapter 2. Book III. Wash drawing.
   Chapter 3. Book III. Water colors.
   Chapter 4. Book III. Pen drawing.
   Chapter 5. Book III. The human head and figure.
   Chapters 6, 7 and 8. Book III. Designing.
   Chapters 9, 10 and 11. Book III. Constructive drawing.

AUGSBURG'S DRAWING.

CHAPTER I.

THE PERSPECTIVE PRINCIPLE.

Aim.— *The aim in this chapter is to show how to represent an object on a flat surface in a given place.*

Materials.— The materials necessary for the work are:
1. A soft pencil. 2. A rubber eraser. 3. A quantity of paper.
4. Round objects for models.

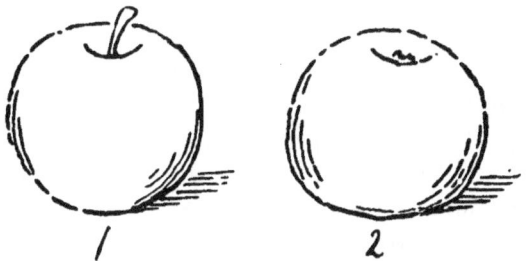

Procure for models three nice round apples; place one on the table before you, and compare it with Fig. 1. Try to see on the apple each point represented in the drawing; turn the apple over and observe the blossom end in the same manner, comparing it with Fig. 2. *The apple gives the idea; the drawing shows how to represent the idea.* Work the following exercises:

1. Draw an apple with the stem pointing upward. Fig. 1.
2. Draw an apple with the stem pointing to the right.
3. Draw an apple with the stem pointing to the left.
4. Draw an apple with the blossom end upward. Fig. 2.
5. Draw an apple with the blossom end to the left.

6. Draw an apple with the blossom end downward.
7. Draw a large apple and place a smaller one on each side.

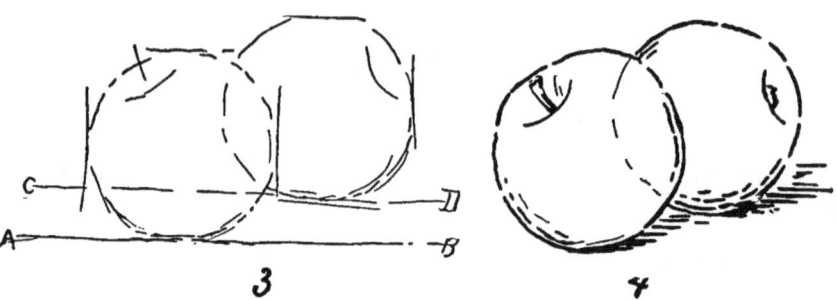

Place two apples on the table before you, as in Fig. 4; observe (1) that the nearest apple shuts from view part of the one back of it; (2) that the lower edge of the first apple is lower than the lower edge of the apple back of it — that they are on different horizontal lines. Observe these two points both in the drawing and on the real apples.

Let your pencil rest on the top of the farther apple, and note that the nearer one appears lower.

When drawing these objects, sketch in with *light lines* the entire form, as shown in Fig. 3, and then finish as in Fig. 4. Light lines to show where the object rests, to mark its height and width, are very helpful. *Draw the lines so light that it will not be necessary to erase them in the finished drawing.* Do not form the habit of erasing. Erasing is seldom necessary.

When doing the following exercises, arrange apples or similar objects before you in the position called for in the exercise. This will enable you to see clearly what you are doing. It is the office of the model to perfect the idea, to make clear the image which you wish to represent. *Always place the idea first.* The idea is the strongest possible incentive; the drawings are not simply to copy, but are to show how to represent the idea.

DRILL EXERCISES.

8. Draw an apple and place another behind and to the right of it. (Fig. 4.)

9. Draw an apple and place another behind and to the left of it.

10. Draw an apple and place one behind and to the right, and one behind and to the left.

11. Draw an apple and place another behind it.

12. Draw an apple and place one in front and to the right, and one in front and to the left.

13. Draw an apple and place three apples around it.

14. Draw an apple and place four apples around it.

The farther away an object, the smaller it should be drawn, and the lines which represent it should be lighter.

15. Draw a row of four apples extending away and to the right.

16. Draw a row of five apples extending away and to the left.

17. Draw an apple and place another some distance beyond.

18. Draw four apples, each one some distance beyond the one in front.

20   AUGSBURG'S DRAWING.

19. Draw an apple and place one some distance in front and one some distance behind.

20. Draw a post and place a ball this side of it and one beyond it.
21. Draw a post and place a ball to the right and one to the left of it.
22. Draw a post and place a ball on top and three balls around it.
23. Draw a post and place four balls about it.
24. Draw a post and place a circle of balls around it.
25. Draw a post and place the most *pleasing* arrangement of balls around it you can represent.
26. Draw a lemon and place lemons on the two marks.
27. Draw a lemon and place two apples behind it.
28. Draw a lemon, an apple, and a sphere in a group.
29. Draw a pear and place pears on the three marks.
30. Draw a pleasing group composed of a lemon, a pear, and an apple.

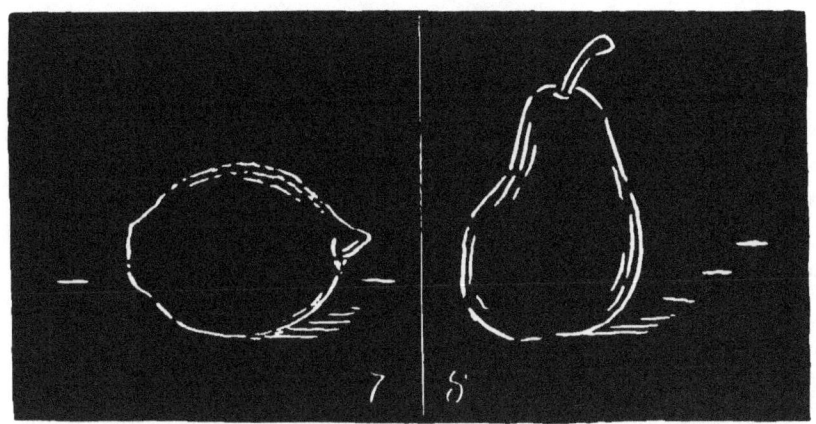

31. Draw a group of four potatoes close together.
32. Draw a group of five potatoes somewhat scattered.
33. Draw a group composed of a ball, a potato, and an apple.

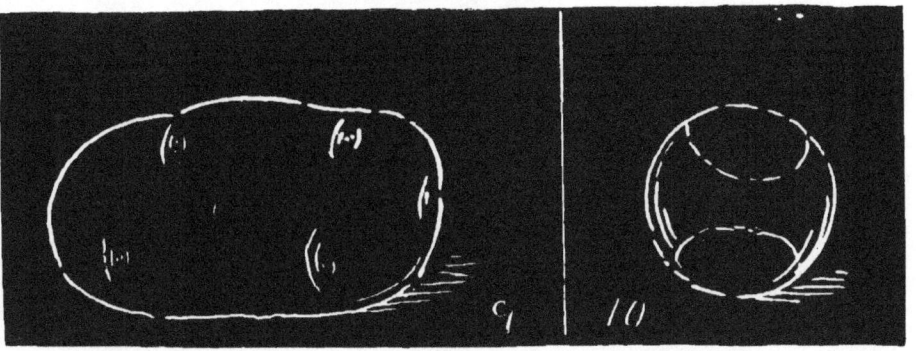

Place, Size, and Character.—There are three elements to be looked for in a drawing: (1) *The place.* (2) *The size, or proportion.* (3) *The character.*

Indicate the place in the drawing where the object is to rest by a mark: the size and proportion by height and width lines, as in Fig. 3.

By character is meant all the higher qualities, such as feeling, expression, action, likeness, life, spirit — qualities that are absorbed rather than taught. Place and size are the letter, and character is the spirit. We can teach the letter, but while teaching it the spirit should be absorbed through example, practice, and general environment.

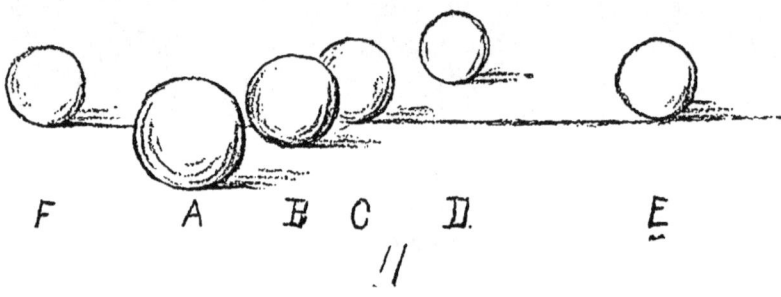

In Fig. 11 the balls are of the same size, but in different places; that is, different distances away. Ball A is drawn larger than Ball B, because it is nearer. Ball D is drawn smaller than Ball A because farther away. Balls C, E, and F are drawn the same size because they are the same distance away — are on the same horizontal line.

Observe in Fig. 11 that the higher up in the picture the object, the farther it appears away.

The Judgment.— In drawing, the position and size of the object should be based on the judgment. If mechanical devices, such as the laws of perspective and comparison are used, they should always be subordinated to this judgment. *The drawing is to be judged by its looks.* If it looks right to the draughtsman, it is to be taken for granted that it is right; and so far as he is concerned, this is so, until he reaches a higher level — until his ideal shows him that it is wrong.

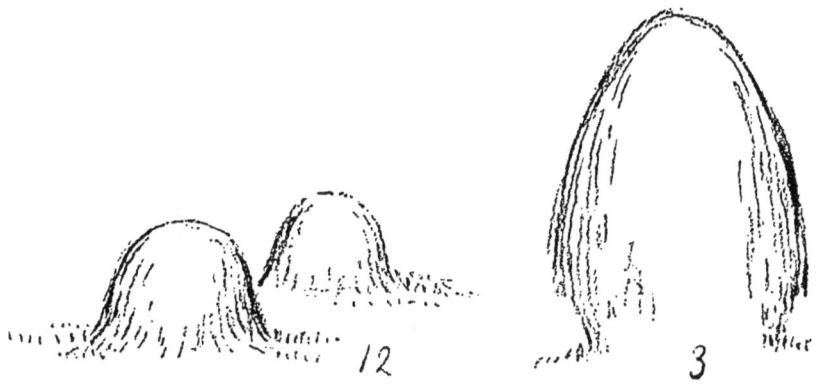

DRILL EXERCISES.

34. Draw Fig. 11.
35. Draw a group of haycocks similar to the group of balls in Fig. 11.
36. Draw a group of haycocks similar to the apples in Fig. 4.
37. Draw five haycocks similar in position to the apples in Fig. 5.
38. Draw a haystack and place a haycock by the side of it.
39. Draw a haystack and place four haycocks around it.
40. Draw a tree and a haystack together.
41. Draw a tree and place another beyond it.
42. Draw a tree and place two others beyond it.
43. Draw a row of four trees extending away.
44. Draw a tree and place a haycock at the right of it.
45. Draw a group containing a tree, haycock, and haystack.
46. Draw two haystacks similar in position to the apples in Fig. 4.

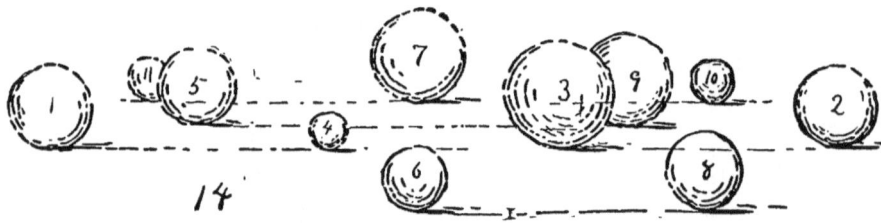

If objects are of the same size, then the farther away they appear the smaller they should be represented in the drawing, and the nearer the objects the larger they should be drawn. (See Fig. 11.)

If, however, the objects are not of the same size, this rule does not apply. In Fig. 14 the balls are of different sizes. Balls 1, 2, 3, and 4 are the same distance away, and are, therefore, shown on the same horizontal line. Ball 5 is farther away, and is, therefore, represented higher in the drawing; and ball 6 must be nearer because it is placed lower in the drawing. This is always true of drawings of objects on a horizontal surface below the level of the eye. Balls 6 and 8 are the same distance away, also balls 5 and 9 and balls 7, 10, and 11.

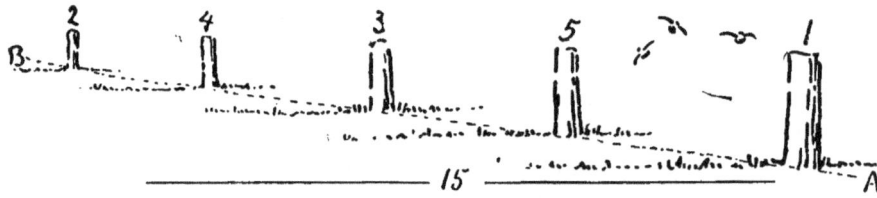

Fig. 15 represents a row of five posts placed at about equal distances apart. They may be used as a means of drill as follows:

Draw on the blackboard a light line as A, B.

At A draw post 1, and at B draw post 2, smaller than post 1. Let the pupils make a similar drawing on their tablets or the blackboard.

Let the pupils draw post 3, without aid, half way between posts 1 and 2 ; post 4 half way between posts 3 and 2, and post 5 half-way between posts 1 and 3.

DRILL EXERCISES.

47. Draw Fig. 15, as directed above. Draw a ball about one-half as high as the post at the left of post 1. At the left of post 5, post 3, post 4, post 2. Draw a ball at the right of post 5, post 4, post 3, post 2, post 1. Place a second ball at the left of post 1, post 5, post 3, post 4, post 2.

48. Draw a row of balls in the same manner as the posts in Fig. 15. Place another ball back of each ball in the row.

49. Draw a row of haycocks in the same manner as the posts in Fig. 15.

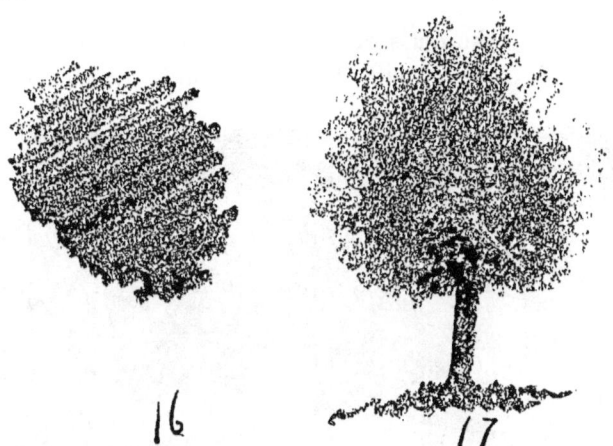

The Drawing of Trees.—The easiest and quickest way of representing trees is as follows :

1. With a soft, blunt pencil mark in the mass of the tree as in Fig. 16,

2. Then with a shorter stroke mark in the branches, softening the edges and aiming to show the general character of the outline, as in Fig. 17. *Work from the center outward.*

The center of the tree is the trunk. *When drawing trees, the foliage and branches should spring from the trunk center outward and upward*, as in Fig. 17. This is one of the most important laws of foliage representation and should be followed, or the unity of the tree will be destroyed and it will look like a heap of rubbish.

In drawing, distance lessens (1) the size of the object; (2) the distinctness of the object; (3) the number of details seen in the object. The farther away an object, the smaller it is drawn, the lighter the line used in representing it, and the less the details show. Observe this in all these drawings, and then observe real trees.

When drawing the mass of the tree on the blackboard, *use the side of a short piece of crayon.* If the crayon is grasped with *three*

MAPLE TREES

fingers and the thumb a line can be made varying in width from the full length of the crayon to a fine line, by merely *tilting the crayon in the hand*.

The process of drawing the trees on the blackboard is the same as with the pencil on paper, and on account of the width of the marks is more rapid. Mark in the mass as in Fig. 16, and then finish as in Fig. 17. Fig. 18 represents the maple both with and without the foliage. Observe in the tree without the foliage that the ends of the limbs are drawn with a lighter line.

Remember, we cannot represent *all* details in drawing. We cannot represent everything we see. For instance, we cannot

represent all the limbs and leaves of a tree, and it is not essential that we should; but *we should aim to represent something*. Here let us aim to represent one, and only one essential feature — *the form*. If we try to represent the light and shade as well as form, we will probably fail, but if we aim at the form alone our success is almost sure. We will try to represent the tree in only one shade or value, as it is seen when between the observer and the light, or as it appears on a cloudy, foggy, smoky, or hazy day. Figs. 19 to 24 are examples.

Trees conform to the same law, and for our purposes, may be used in the same manner as balls, posts, haycocks, etc.

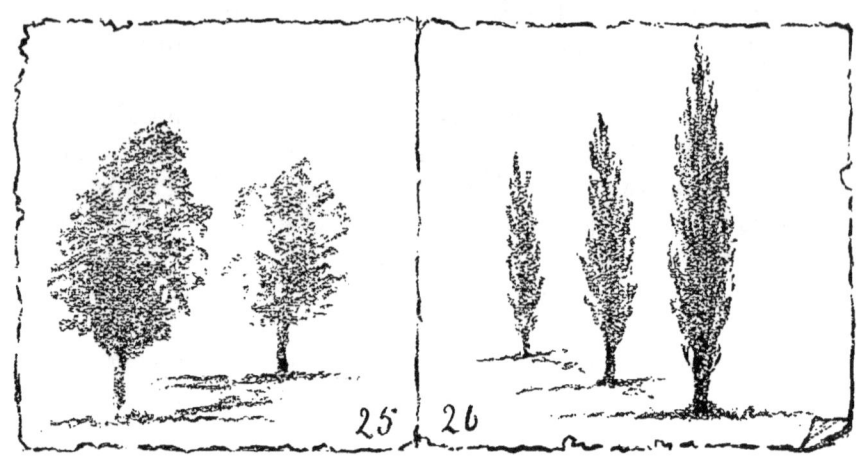

In Fig. 25 the second tree is represented farther away by simply placing it higher in the picture, and drawing it smaller, the same as with the balls. Fig. 26 carries out the same idea with three trees.

DRILL EXERCISES.

50. Draw a tree, then draw another tree farther away.
51. Draw a group of three trees different distances away.
52. Draw a group of five trees different distances away.
53. Draw a group of six trees, similar to tree 19, different distances away.
54. Draw eight trees different distances away, similar to trees 19 and 20; similar to trees 21 and 22; similar to trees 22, 23, and 24.
55. Draw a row of trees after the manner of the posts in Fig. 15.
56. Draw a row of trees after the manner of the posts in Fig. 15, and place a haycock at the left of each tree.

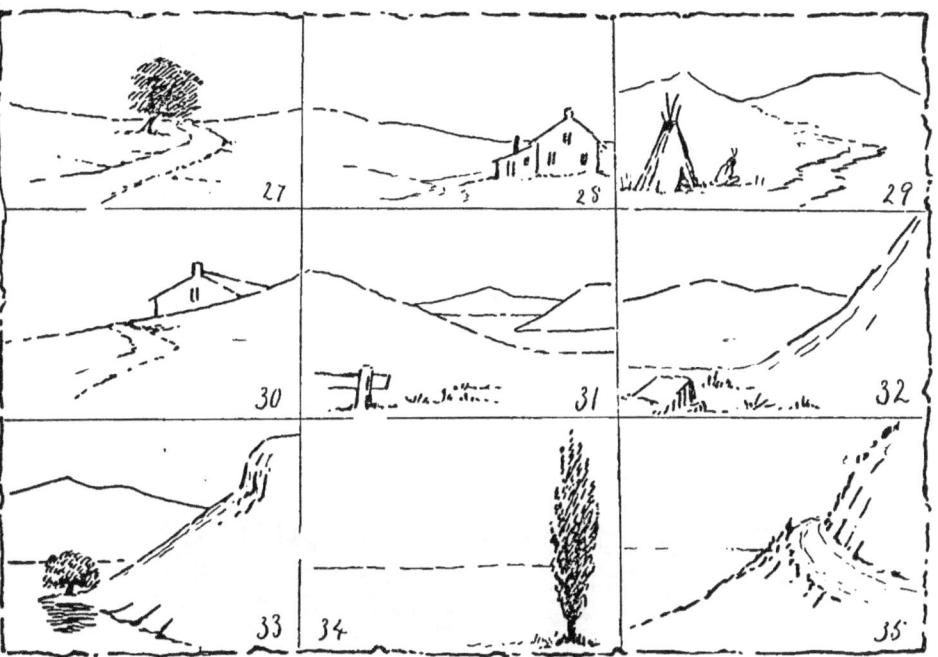

Figs. 27–35 represent simple landscapes into which trees are to be introduced, according to the suggestions given below. Each landscape contains an object with which the size of the trees may be compared.

A good plan is to draw one of these landscapes on the blackboard. Let the pupils draw a similar one on their tablets, and introduce trees as given below.

DRILL EXERCISES.

57. Introduce into Sketch 27 four trees at different distances away.

58. In Fig. 28 place trees back of the house and four trees at the left of the road.

59. Introduce six trees into Fig. 29.

60. Introduce trees back of the house in Fig. 30, and three trees at the left of the path.

61. Introduce into Fig. 31 six trees.

62. Introduce five trees into Fig. 32.

63. Introduce into Fig. 33 eight trees.

64. Introduce twelve trees into Fig. 34, at various distances away. (See Fig. 26.)

65. Introduce trees into Fig. 35, after the manner of Fig. 36.

Suggestions in Teaching.— The first aim of the teacher should be to teach the mechanical process of representing the object on a flat surface. To do this, objects should be chosen

AUGSBURG'S DRAWING.   31

with which the pupils are familiar, such as balls, apples, and similar objects.

1. Teach the pupils how to represent the object on a flat surface. This can best be done from the blackboard with spheres as in Fig. 11.

2. Teach the perspective principle — how to represent the object in different positions — near and far away, to the right, left, in front, and back of a given object or place. Spheres are the best for this work. Use the model or object when teaching; use it persistently. The model is the principle source of the idea — of the mental image which the pupil reproduces. The progress of the class will be more rapid, more satisfactory, and more complete when the model is used than when it is not.

Using the model does not necessarily imply drawing from the model. We may use the model and not draw from it at all. We use the model to gain ideas of form, ideas of relation, ideas of construction, ideas of proportion, all of which perfect the mental image and make it vivid and strong.

CHAPTER II.

The Box as a Type Form.

It is the aim in this and the following chapter to show methods of teaching the principle of representing *distance away*, or the *third dimension*, on a flat surface.

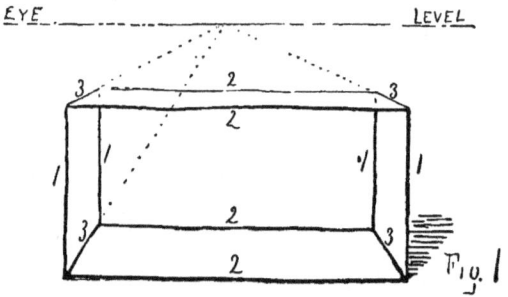

Procure for models several pasteboard boxes of about the proportion of Fig. 1. Place one of these boxes before you in the position of Fig. 1, and observe:

1. The four *vertical* lines, 1, 1, 1, 1.
2. The four *horizontal* lines 2, 2, 2, 2.
3. The four *horizontal receding* lines, 3, 3, 3, 3.
4. Observe that there are *three distinct sets of lines with four lines in each set, viz.*: A set of four vertical lines, a set of four horizontal lines, and a set of four horizontal receding lines.
5. Observe that the vertical lines in the drawing are drawn parallel with the sides of the paper on which the drawing is made; the horizontal lines parallel with the top and bottom of the paper; and that the horizontal receding lines converge to a point.

The horizontal receding lines on the model converge in the same manner as represented in the drawing, but it is difficult for the untrained eye to see this convergence. The point to which these lines converge is the *center of vision*.

The Center of Vision is an imaginary point directly opposite the eye. *All horizontal receding lines converge to this point.*

E L (eye level) in Fig. 1 is the *Horizon Line*. The horizon line in drawing is the line that marks the *level of the eye*. It is the level-of-the-eye line. The center of vision being the point directly opposite the eye *is always in the horizon line*. Objects drawn below the horizon line are said to be drawn below the level of the eye, and those above this line, above the level of the eye.

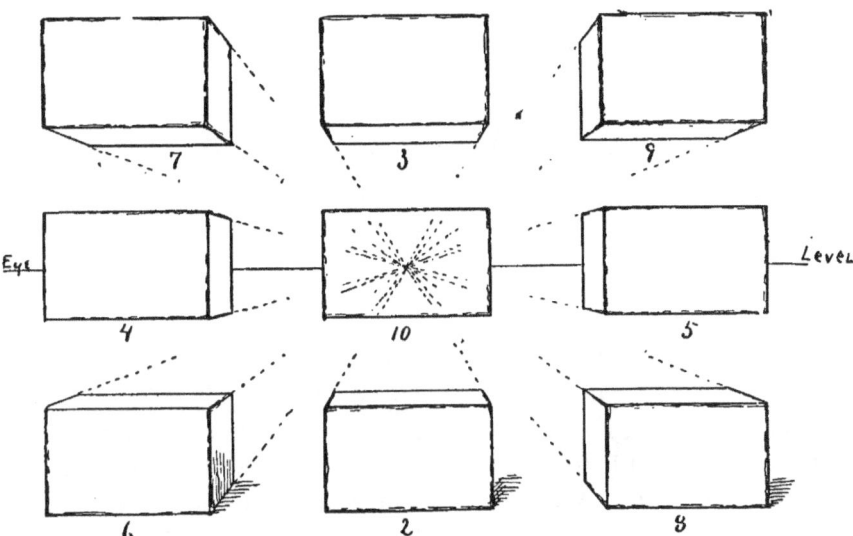

Using the vertical, horizontal, and horizontal receding lines, the box may be drawn in nine positions, *viz.*:

Below the eye, Fig. 2.
Above the eye, Fig. 3.

At the left of the eye, Fig. 4.
At the right of the eye, Fig. 5.
Below and at the left of the eye, Fig. 6.
Above and at the left of the eye, Fig. 7.
Below and at the right of the eye, Fig. 8.
Above and at the right of the eye, Fig. 9.
Directly in front of the eye, Fig 10.

Hold a box in each of the above positions and compare it with the drawing, face by face and line by line.

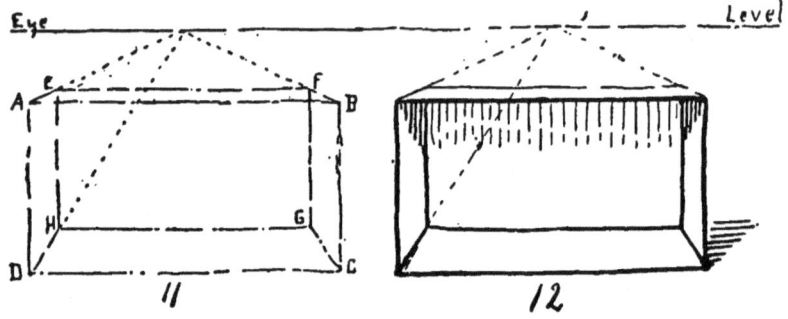

The box is drawn as follows:

1. Draw the front face, A B C D, Fig. 11. (2) Choose the center of vision. (3) From the points A, B, and D draw receding lines to the center of vision. (4) Choose the point E and draw the remaining lines. Draw first with very light lines as in Fig. 11 and then finish with heavier as in Fig. 12. *Do not use a ruler or straight edge at all.* Make the drawings about 2½ inches long and 1 inch high. On the blackboard the drawings should be at least 12x7 inches.

Use the model continually. The model is to aid and perfect the mental image — the thought — the idea which is to be reproduced.

Drill should follow representation. The order is, (1) the idea, (2) how to represent the idea, (3) drill exercise.

DRILL EXERCISES.

1. Draw a box below the eye.
2. Draw a box above the eye.
3. Draw a box at the left of the eye.
4. Draw a box at the right of the eye.
5. Draw a box below and at the left of the eye.
6. Draw a box below and at the right of the eye.
7. Draw a box above and at the left of the eye.
8. Draw a box above and at the right of the eye.
9. Draw a box directly in front of the eye.

After drawing a box, compare it with the model. Do this, not so much to see if it is like the box, as to see if you have the principle correct. The box or model shows the idea, the drawing how to represent the idea. Refer all of your difficulties to your model.

10. Draw a box below the level of the eye. Remove the top face. Fig. 13.
11. Draw a box below the eye. Remove the top face. Remove the back face.

12. Draw a box below the eye. Remove the top face. Remove the right face.

If you cannot see how the above is done, remove the top and right faces from your pasteboard box and see.

13. Draw a box below the eye. Remove the top face. Remove the left face. Remove the back face.

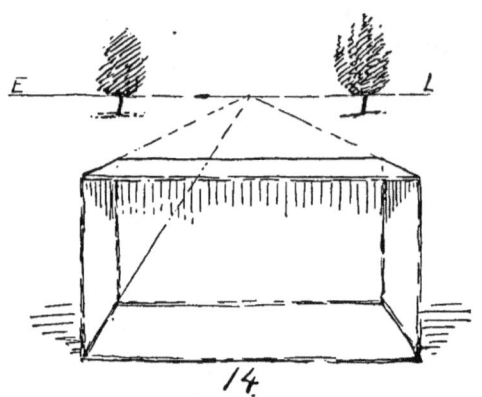

14. Draw a box below the eye. Remove the front face. (Fig. 14.)

15. Draw a box below the eye. Remove the front, right, and back faces. (The left, top, and bottom faces will remain.)

16. Draw a box below the eye and remove the front, top, and back faces.

17. Draw a box below the eye and remove the front, bottom, and back faces.

18. Draw a box at the left of the eye. Remove the front face. Remove the back face. (Fig. 15.)

19. Draw a box at the left of the eye. Remove the front, right, and back faces. Place two apples inside the box.

20. Draw a box at the left of the eye. Remove the front,

bottom, and back faces. Place an apple on top of the box, one at the left and one at the right.

21. Draw a box at the right of the eye and remove the front, right, and back faces.

22. Draw a box at the right of the eye and remove the front, top, and back faces. Place a ball in front.

23. Draw two boxes, one at the left and one at the right of the same center of vision. Remove from each the front, left, and back faces. Place four balls in front.

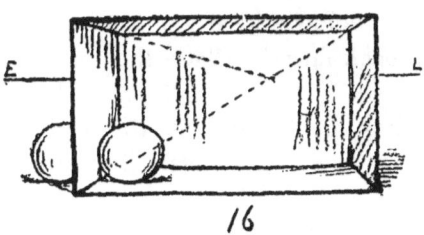

24. Draw a box directly in front of the eye and remove the front face. (Fig. 16.)

25. Draw a box directly in front of the eye and remove the front, left, and back faces. Place a ball on top and one back of the box.

26. Draw a box directly in front of the eye and remove the front, bottom, and back faces. Place two balls on opposite sides and touching the right face.

27. Draw a box directly in front of the eye and remove the front, right, and left faces.

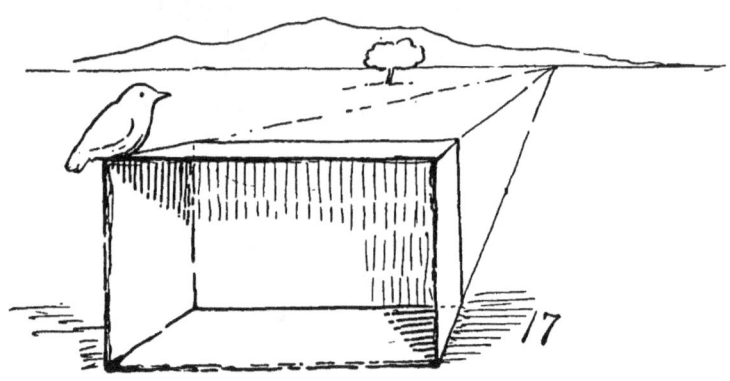

28. Draw a box below and at the left of the eye and remove the front face. (Fig. 17.)

29. Draw a box below and at the left of the eye and remove the front, top, and back faces. Place the bird on the farther left corner.

30. Draw a box below and at the right of the eye and remove the front, top, and back faces. Place the bird on the farther right corner.

31. Draw two boxes using the same center of vision, one below and at the right and one below and at the left of the eye. Remove from each the front, bottom, and back faces.

32. Draw a box above and at the left of the eye and remove the bottom face.

33. Draw a box above and at the right of the eye and remove the front face.

34. Draw a box above the eye and remove the front, right, and left faces.

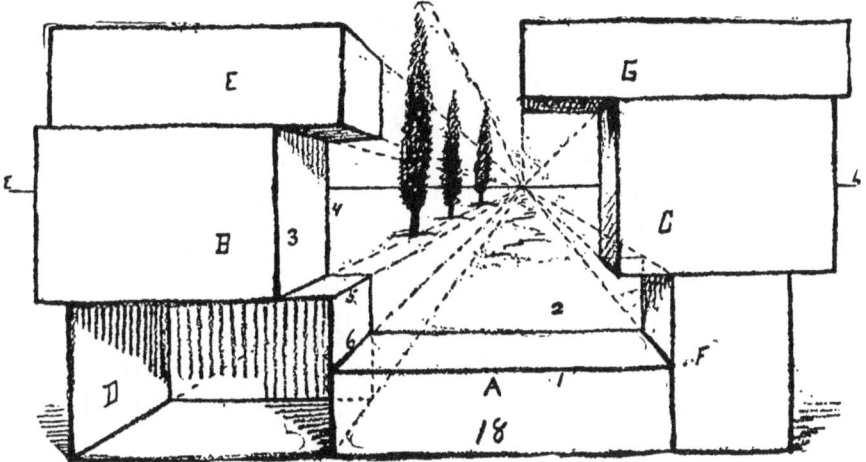

Draw Fig. 18 on the blackboard. Use it as a drill exercise as follows:

1. Henry, pass to the blackboard. Point to a vertical line. Point to three vertical lines. Point to six vertical lines. Point to two parallel vertical lines. Point to three parallel vertical lines; to six. Hold your pointer in a vertical position. Find a vertical line in the room.

2. Mary may take the pointer and point to a horizontal line in the drawing. To three horizontal lines. To seven horizontal lines. Point to two parallel horizontal lines. To four parallel horizontal lines; to six. Hold the pointer in a horizontal position. Hold your arms horizontal. Find a horizontal line in the room. Each pupil may point to a horizontal line on his desk.

3. Joseph, what is the meaning of *receding?* Illustrate. Take the pointer and point to a receding line in the drawing; to another. Point to ten receding lines in the drawing. Hold your pointer in a receding position. Hold your pointer in a horizontal position. In a horizontal receding position. Find a receding line in the room.

4. Agnes, where is the center of vision in the drawing? Point to a box below the level of the eye. At the left of the eye. At the right. Below and at the left. Below and at the right. Above and at the left. Above and at the right.

5. Each pupil may take his box and hold it in the position of box A. Point to line 1 on your box. Line 2. Line 6. Hold your box in the position of box B. Point to line 4. Hold your box in the position of box C. Box D. Box E. Box F. Box G.

6. Charles, which represents the longer edge, line 1 or 2? Measure with your pointer line 2 and compare it with the length of line 1. Why is line 2 drawn shorter than line 1? Which represents the longer edge, line 3 or line 4? Measure with your pointer line 4 and compare it with line 3. Why is line 3 drawn longer than line 4? Line 5 and line 6 represent parallel lines and are of the same length. All of the receding lines you see in these boxes are parallel and of the same length.

7. John, point to the line that represents the level of the eye. Why can you see the bottom of box G? Why does the top of box A show? Why can you see the right face of box B? Point to the tallest tree in the drawing. The shortest. (The farther tree is the tallest and the middle tree the shortest.)

Suggestions in Teaching.— Each pupil should have a small paste-board box for a model. This box may be procured at home or made from a strip cut from the end of the drawing paper. Cut a strip of drawing paper one inch wide and about six inches long. Fold this strip as shown in Fig. 19 and fasten with a pin or mucilage. This will make a very serviceable model with the top and bottom faces removed.

The uses the pupil may make of his model are as follows:

1. To illustrate in concrete form the nine positions of the box as they are represented in the drawings. Figs. 2–10.

2. To varify the different points made in the drawing, such as the different classes of lines, and the removal of faces.

3. To use as the source of the idea, the source from which the pupil is to find the points he wishes to represent in his drawing.

The greatest difficulty to be overcome by the teacher is to lead the pupil to use his model intelligently; to so teach him that he will seek the model rather than the teacher when in need of information.

When teaching use both model and drawing. Use the model as the source of the idea, use the drawing to show how to represent the idea on a flat surface; use the model to make clear the drawing, use the drawing to make clear the model. If the pupil does not know how to represent the top face of the box he is drawing, it is difficult, if not quite impossible, to tell him by word of mouth. He must be shown both in the drawing and by means of the model.

Draw on the Blackboard.— Many pupils will gain the idea and learn the principle more rapidly by seeing some one else draw, than by any other method. Frequently draw or have one of the pupils draw on the blackboard a drawing similar to the following. Let the drawing be made without comment and if possible to the accompaniment of low music.

Draw a box below and at the left of the eye. Draw two or three trees in the distance. Remove from the box the top face. The back face. The left face. Add the back face. Add the left face. Add the top face. Remove the front face. Remove the right face. Remove the back face. Add the back face. Add the right face. Remove the top face. Remove the back face. Add the back face. Add the top face. Place a ball on the top face. Place two balls inside of the box, etc.

Blackboard Drawing.— The blackboard is the most satisfactory place for drill exercises. Divide the pupils into divisions, and have a division draw at the blackboard each day.

Teaching by Groups.— Teach the position of the boxes in groups of four each, as follows :

First group: Boxes below, above, at the left, and at the right of the eye. Fig. 2, 3, 4 and 5.

Second group: Boxes below and at the left, below and at the right, above and at the left, and above and at the right of the eye. Fig. 6, 7, 8 and 9.

The box directly in front of the eye may be taught by itself or included in either group.

Length of Drawing Period.— The drawing period should be of such a length as to give from ten to fifteen minutes of actual drawing each day. This is far better than a long period two or three times per week. Drawing is not slow work. If the pupil understands what he is to do the execution is very rapid. A great deal of drawing can be done in ten minutes.

SCIENTIFIC AND EYE PERSPECTIVE.— There are two methods of teaching drawing, which may be called *scientific perspective* and *eye perspective*.

The first takes advantage of certain lines, points and laws which are approximately correct for the purpose of *revealing the principle of receding surfaces and teaching how to represent them*. The second method is simply drawing the object as it appears to the eye.

The first is addressed to the mind through the reasoning powers, the second to the mind through the perceptive powers.

Many draughtsmen object to scientific perspective on the ground that it is not true under all conditions, but this may be said also of eye perspective. Drawing is at its best not an exact science. It is a series of compromises from beginning to end. It is but an imperfect interpreter of ideas.

Scientific perspective should not be rejected because it is not perfect, but should be used for that which it is best adapted to teach. The two methods are mutually helpful, one revealing the *principle*, and the other the *appearance* of form. The first is adapted to conceptive, or thought, drawing; the second, to perceptive, or object drawing. Both have their place and use, and both together are far more complete than either taken separately.

In this book both kinds of drawing are used, but both are used as a means to an end, not as an end in themselves.

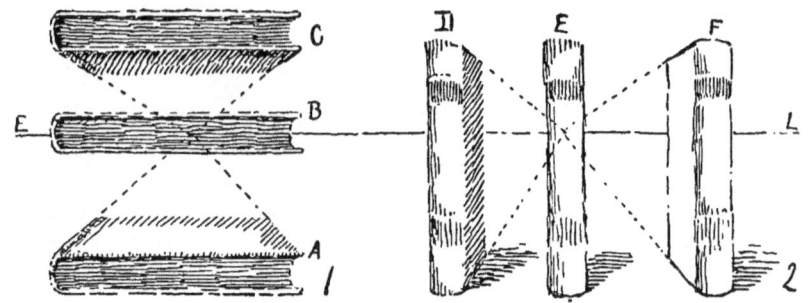

CHAPTER III.

THE CUBE AS A TYPE FORM.

Definitions. — *For what purpose is the horizon line used in drawing?* (1) The horizon line is used to mark the level of the eye. (2) It is to show whether the top or bottom of horizontal surfaces can be seen and approximately how wide they should be drawn.

Hold a book in your hand below the level of the eye and at easy arm's length away as in A Fig. 1. You can see the top. Hold it above the eye as at C and you can see the bottom. Hold it on a level with the eye as at B and you can see neither the top nor bottom. This place where neither the top nor bottom of the book can be seen is the level of the eye, and is marked by the horizon line.

Standing on a plain or the shore of a large body of water, this line can be plainly seen as dividing the earth and sky. We can tell that it is on a level with the eye by the same means used in Fig. 1.

It is by the level of the eye that we judge either consciously or unconsciously the position of objects vertically.

For what purpose is the center of vision used in drawing? (1) It is used to mark in the horizon line the point directly oppo-

44

site the eye. (2) To show the *right or left* faces of objects can be seen. (3) To show where horizontal receding lines vanish.

Hold a book in your hand at the left of the eye as at D Fig. 2, and you will see the right face of the book. Hold it at the right of the eye as at F, and the left face is seen. Hold it at a point directly in front of the eye as at E (close one eye), and neither face shows. The point in the horizon line that marks this position is the Center of Vision.

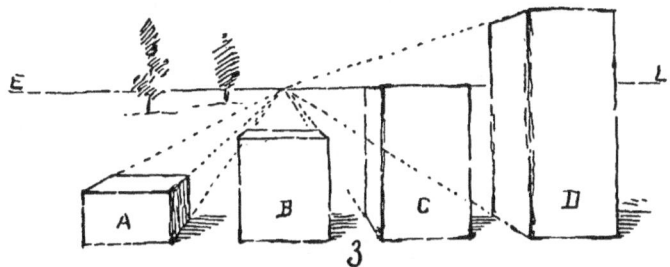

We see the top of blocks A and B, Fig. 3, because they are below the horizon line (level of the eye). The top of the block C is on a level with the eye and the top of block D is above the level of the eye, hence their tops cannot be seen. We can see the right face of block A because it is at the left of the eye. We can see the left face of blocks C and D, because they are at the right of the eye. We cannot see either the right or left face of block B, because it is directly below the eye.

In Fig. 4 the top of stumps A and B show because they are below the level of the eye (horizon line). The top of stump C cannot be seen because it is on a level with the eye and the top of stump D cannot be seen because it is above the eye. The left end of log E can be seen because it is at the right of the eye. The right end of log F can be seen because it is at the left of the eye. Neither end of log G can be seen because it is directly below the eye.

What receding lines vanish at the center of vision? Horizontal receding lines; that is, lines that pass directly away from you, and are parallel with the surface of the earth. All the receding lines that have been used thus far are horizontal receding.

Is the horizon line a fixed line, and is the center of vision a fixed point? No, your horizon line changes as you change. If you are standing on a plain, your horizon line (level of the eye) is low down. If you ascend a hill or mountain, it rises with you.

The center of vision changes right or left in the horizon line as your eye changes. It is always opposite the eye.

Is it always necessary to use the horizon line and the center of vision in drawing? No. They are merely aids, and may be used or not at pleasure. When drawing conceptively they are very useful, but when drawing perceptively (that is, from the object) they are not so useful. Their greatest use is in assisting the mind to judge correctly the relation of certain objects arranged perspectively. They are, and should always be, subordinate in their function. They are servants of the mind.

What is the difference between the center of vision and the "eye"? They are opposite points, but are represented in the drawing by the same point. The center of vision is the point opposite the eye, and the eye is the point opposite the center of vision. The eye is referred to when reference is made to a point this side of the object, and the center of vision is referred to when the point is beyond the object. For example, in Fig. 1, book A is below the level of the eye. The center of vision is beyond book A.

What do receding lines represent in drawing? Distance away.

Are parallel receding lines drawn parallel? No. They converge to a point; but they do in reality represent parallel lines, and are called parallel in the drawing.

NOTE.— It is often urged against the use of the center of vision that a box cannot be seen outside of this point, say below and at the left of the eye, as in Fig. 5; that line 2 being farther away will be shorter than line 1, and lines 3 and 4, instead of being parallel, will converge slightly; that the front of the box would not be a true rectangle; all of which is to a slight degree true, but to such a slight degree that the eye cannot detect the error when the object is placed a suitable distance away. The difference is more theoretical than practical.

Figs. 5 and 6 represent a photograph of two boxes, one below and at the left of the eye and one below and at the right, yet neither of them show any of the above errors. The final test, however, must rest with the mind through the feeling and judgment.

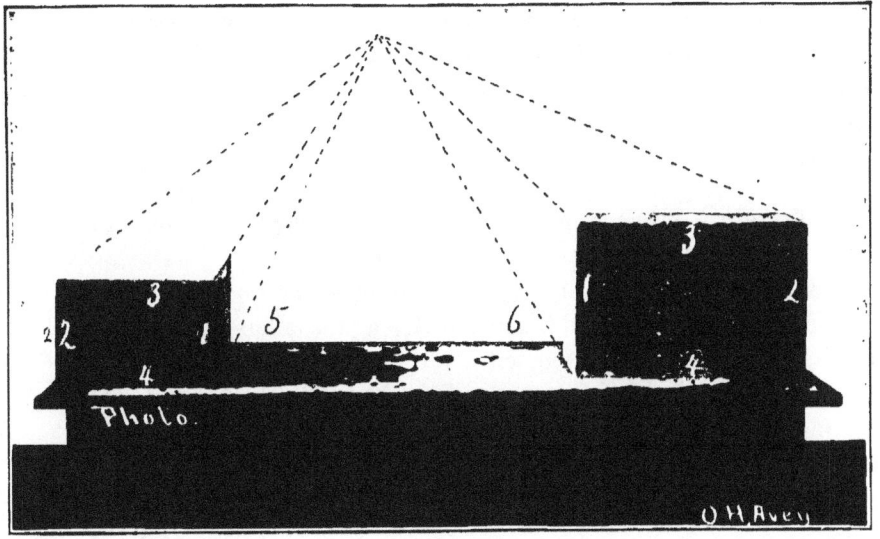

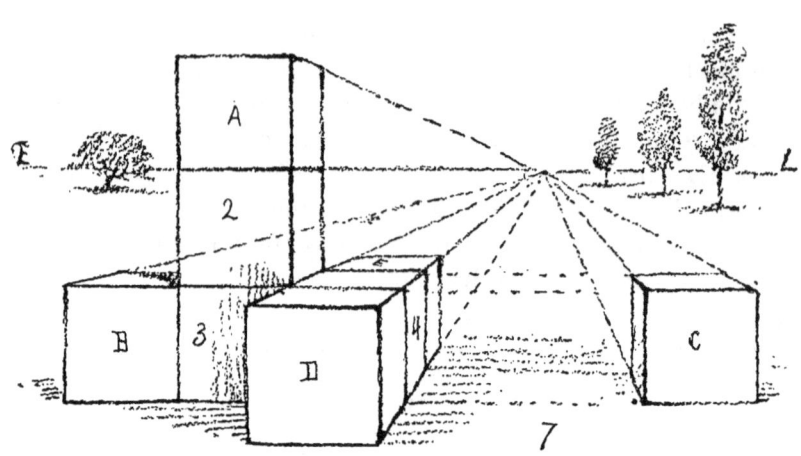

Placing Cubes.— Figs. 8, 9 and 10 represent three groups of four cubes each. Fig. 8 represents the *receding group*. It is called receding because in removing the cubes the receding lines predominate. For a similar reason, Fig. 9 represents the *vertical group*, and Fig. 10 the *horizontal group*. The purpose in this lesson is the placing of these blocks in various relations to each other. The aim is to enable the pupil to acquire power in associating square-cornered objects together, and to learn how to represent receding surfaces.

Models.—Use for models four cubical blocks. Four crayon boxes make very good models for class use.

In Fig. 7, block 1 has been removed from position in Fig. 8 and placed on block 2 and marked A; again it has been placed at the left of block 3 and marked B; then two blocks to the right of block 4 and marked C; then in front of block 4 as at D and behind block 4 as at E.

Make the following observations in Fig. 7:
1. Observe how much shorter the receding distances are

than the vertical and horizontal distances. All receding distances are and should be judged by the unaided eye.

2. Observe that the square marked D is larger than the squares marked 2 and 3. This is because the cube has been moved nearer.

3. Block B is about as far to the left as it is allowable to be placed and use the center of vision; a further distance would place it out of the range of vision and make it distorted.

4. Blocks A, B, C, 2, 3 and 4, should be the same size, as they are practically the same distance away.

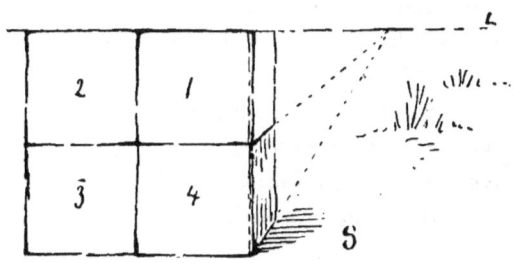

DRILL EXERCISES BASED ON FIG. 8.

1. Remove block 1 and place it on 2.
2. Remove block 1 and place it at the right of 4.
3. Remove block 1 and place it in front of 4.
4. Remove block 1 and place it behind 4.
5. Remove block 1 and place it two blocks to the right of 4.
6. Remove block 2 and place it at the left of 3.
7. Place block 2 on 1, and 3 on 2.
8. Place block 1 at the right of 4, and block 2 at the right of 1.

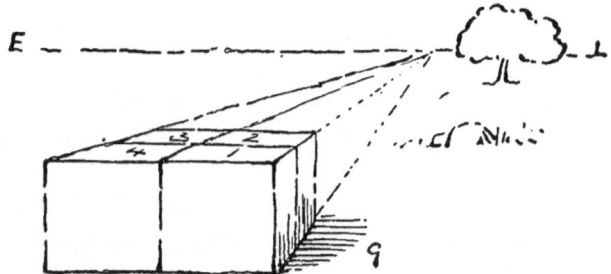

DRILL EXERCISES BASED ON FIG. 9.

9. Remove block 1 and place it on 3.
10. Remove block 2 and place it on 4.
11. Remove blocks 2 and 4 and place them below and at the right of the eye.
12. Place block 1 behind 3, and 2 behind 1.
13. Remove block 1 one block to the right.
14. Remove block 1 one block forward.
15. Separate all the blocks about one-fourth of a block apart.

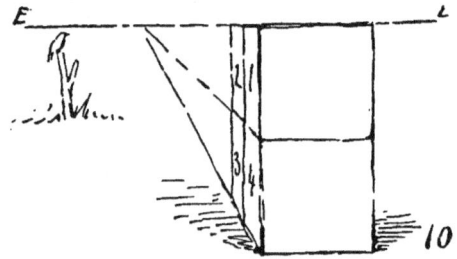

DRILL EXERCISES BASED ON FIG. 10.

16. Remove block 2 and place on 1, and block 3 and place it under 4.
17. Remove block 1 and place it at the left of 3.
18. Remove block 1 one-half of a block to the right.

19. Remove block 2 one-half of a block to the left.
20. Remove block 3 one-half block to the left.
21. Remove block 1 one-half of a block forward, and block 3 one-half of a block back.

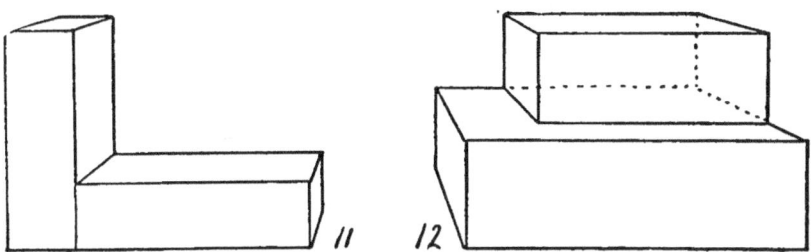

Figs. 11 and 12 represent two very serviceable models that may be used to great advantage at this point.

Fig. 11 is simply two blocks nailed together in the form of an L, and Fig. 12 is a smaller block nailed to a larger one so that one corner and two sides are even.

These models may be drawn in a great number of ways illustrating every phase of this work. Figs. 13-24 represent the different positions in which Fig. 11 may be drawn, below and at the left of the eye.

Manner of Using the Blocks.— The pupil holds one of the blocks in his hand in the position he is to draw it, and from it gets his ideas of proportion, position and facts of detail. The pupil does not make a drawing of the model exactly as it appears to the eye, but represents the facts as they would appear in a given position.

An L shaped model may be made from two blocks, cut from clay, plaster or similar substance.

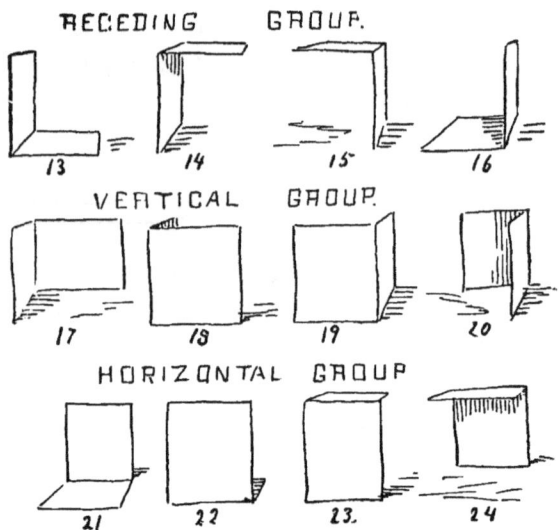

DRILL EXERCISES BASED ON BLOCK 11.

Make the following drawings below and at the left of the eye.
22. Draw the block in the position of Fig. 13.
23. Draw the block in the position of Fig. 14.
24. Draw the block in the position of Fig. 15.
25. Draw the block in the position of Fig. 16.
26. Draw the block in the position of Fig. 17.
27. Draw the block in the position of Fig. 18.
28. Draw the block in the position of Fig. 19.
29. Draw the block in the position of Fig. 20.
30. Draw the block in the position of Fig. 21.
31. Draw the block in the position of Fig. 22.
32. Draw the block in the position of Fig. 23.
33. Draw the block in the position of Fig. 24.

The above problems can be repeated below and at the right of the eye if desired.

In like manner a set of problems may be made with model 12.

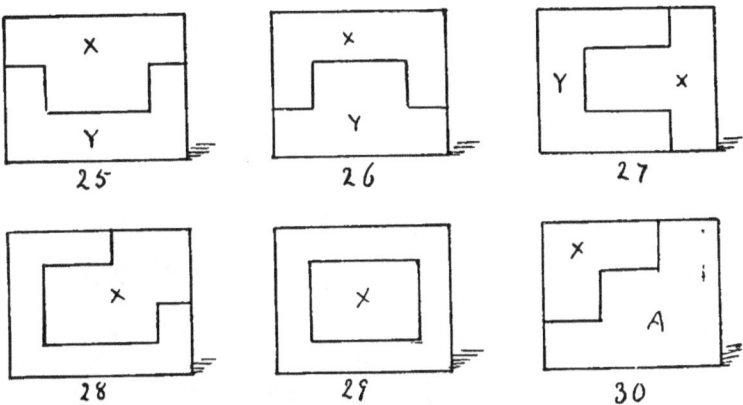

Conceptive Drawing.— Figs. 25–30 are solid blocks drawn directly in front of the eye. On the front face of each block is a part marked X which is to be removed as directed in the problems given below.

This work is to be purely conceptive, and is a test of the understanding of the previous work. If the pupil cannot do this work without a model it is because he does not yet understand the principle and should be drilled on models 11 and 12 until the principle is learned.

DRILL EXERCISE.

34. Draw 26 below the eye and remove the part marked X. (See Y, Fig 31.)

35. Draw 25 below the eye, and remove the part marked X.

36. Draw 25 below and at the left of the eye, and remove the part marked X.

37. Draw 26 below and at the right of the eye, and remove the part marked X.

38. Draw 26 below the eye, and remove the part marked X to above the eye directly over the part marked Y. (See Fig. 31.)

39. Draw Fig. 27 below and at the left of the eye, and remove the part marked X to below and at the right of the eye.

40. Draw 28 below and at the left of the eye, and remove X.

41. Draw 29 below and at the right of the eye, and remove X.

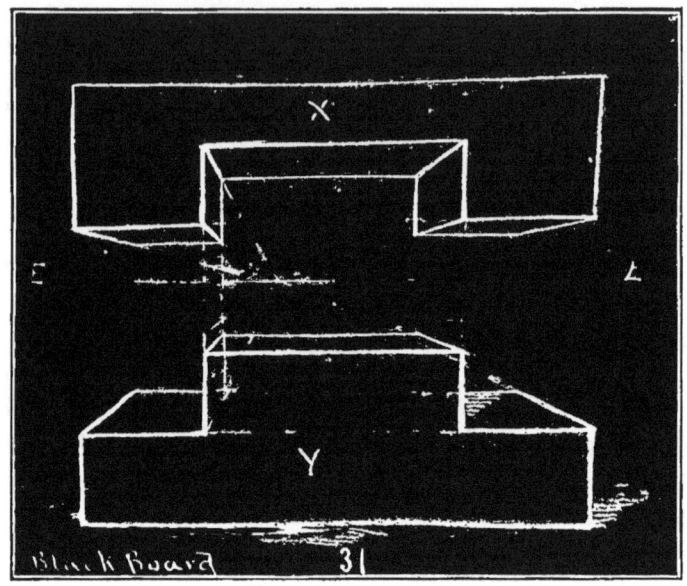

42. Draw 30 below and at the right of the eye, and remove X.

Suggestions in Teaching.—One of the vital points in this work with cubes is to show the pupil how to use his model intelligently. This may be done by requiring the pupil to place the models in the same position as that represented by a drawing on the blackboard. Four crayon boxes are excellent models for this purpose.

AUGSBURG'S DRAWING. 55

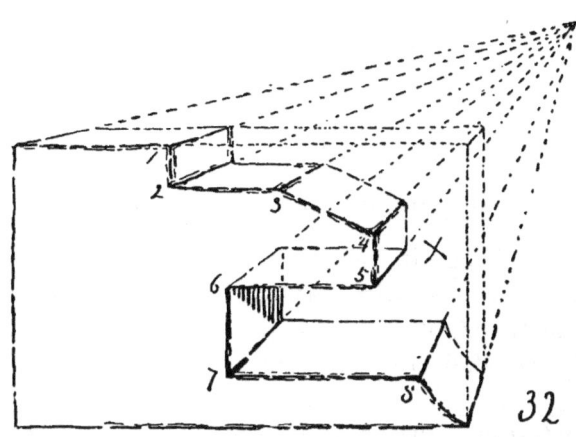

Draw for the Pupils.—Nothing shows the pupils *how* so quickly as drawing for them on the blackboard. This may be done by the teacher or a pupil. The following are excellent drawings for this purpose:

1. Draw a small cube below and at the left of the eye. Add a similar cube to the top face. Add another cube to the top of the last one. Add a cube to the left face of the first cube. Add a cube to the right face. Add a cube to the front face. Add a cube to the back face.

2. Draw a small cube below and at the left of the eye. Draw a similar cube two blocks to the right of it. Two blocks to the left. Two blocks in front. Two blocks back, etc.

Draw a large block similar to Fig. 32 and cut from it the part marked X. Begin cutting away X at point 1 and finish as you go, proceeding in the order of the numbering from 1 to 8.

CHAPTER IV.

Application of the Box Form to Picture Making.

Aim.—The design in this chapter is (1) To show methods of applying the principles already learned to picture making. (2) To present methods of modifying, constructing and changing objects. (3) To show the different kinds of lines and how to use them.

The greatest use that can be made of these drawings is to suggest how similar objects may be drawn.

Copying.—It is the office of the copy to exemplify the method, hence it is always right to copy for the purpose of learning. There is nothing in the object itself to show one how to draw it. This ability must be acquired either by seeing some one draw and imitating him, or by imitating a drawing that has already been made. Most objects contain length, breadth, and thickness. In drawing, the third dimension must be represented in direct opposition to previous experience. How is this to be done except by copying the work of others? It is the abuse of the copy that is wrong; the using of the copy as an end and not as a means to an end; that is, copying without understanding—without an end or motive in view; copying to reproduce another's drawing or picture. Such copying is not educative, but intelligent copying to acquire a principle, or a method, to learn how to represent ideas on a flat surface, is educative. It is doubtful if the average pupil can acquire an ability to draw in any other way. All professions and trades are more or less learned by copying.

Drawing students seek art centers, not because objects are more numerous, but because there are better teachers to show how, and finer pictures to study. How are they to follow these teachers except by imitating the one or copying, either consciously or unconsciously, the other? How can the accumulated knowledge of the world be gotten and used unless we copy it?

If directed properly copying will not lead to mannerism and take away the individuality of the child. The individuality should be made stronger by the knowledge thus acquired. If imitative, imaginative, memory and object drawing are carried along together, there can be no danger from this source.

The following exercises represent a simple yet progressive plan of picture making.

1

In the following drawings the center of vision may be found by the continuation of two or more receding lines to the point of intersection.

Sketch in all drawings with light lines first, and then finish with heavier.

DRILL EXERCISES.

Fig. 1 is a package of paper drawn below the level of the eye. Draw it as follows:
1. Draw Fig. 1.
2. Draw Fig. 1 below and at the left of the eye.

3. Draw Fig. 1 below and at the right of the eye with the folded end to the left.

It is hardly practical to procure a model like the objects represented in each one of these drawings, nor is it desirable to do so; still similar models are very serviceable to show what has been represented and how it has been done. The office of these draw-

ings is to show how, and the highest use that can be made of them is their use in connection with similar objects or models.

Figs. 2–10 are nine baskets drawn in the nine positions of the

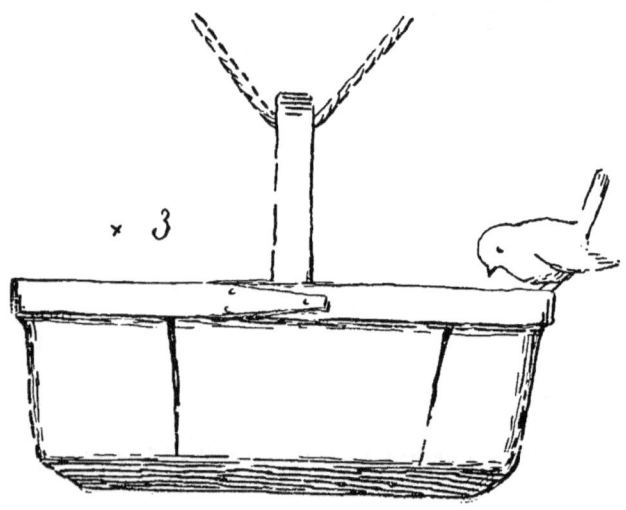

box. Each basket, in addition to being drawn in a different position, is represented as composed of different material showing different treatment. Each basket may be drawn in the nine different positions represented by the box in Chapter I.

Fig. 2 is a pen drawing of a fruit basket drawn below the eye. Draw it as follows:

4. Draw Fig. 2 full of cherries.
5. Draw Fig. 2 bottom face up.

Basket three is drawn above the eye, and as it is not resting on anything, it must be suspended from above. We know it is above the eye because we can see the bottom. It is a pen drawing.

6. Draw Fig. 3.

7. Draw Fig. 3 below the eye resting on the ground.

Basket 4 is drawn at the left of the eye. Observe that the wicker work of which the basket is composed does not extend all over the side, but is merely suggested at one end; the imagination is left to fill out the remainder of the wicker work. *Suggestion* is one of the most important elements in drawing and should receive the closest attention. Observe that the apples in basket 4 are suggested by one stem and one blossom end. Fig. 4 is a pencil drawing and Fig. 5 a pen drawing.

8. Draw basket 4.
9. Draw basket 4 at the right of the eye.
10. Draw basket 5.
11. Draw basket 5 at the left of the eye.

6

Basket six is drawn directly in front of the eye, consequently the front face alone shows. It differs from basket 4 in not having any part suggested but everything represented as it appears on the basket.

12. Draw basket 6 below the eye.

13. Draw basket 6 resting on its side below and at the left of the eye, and five balls rolling out.

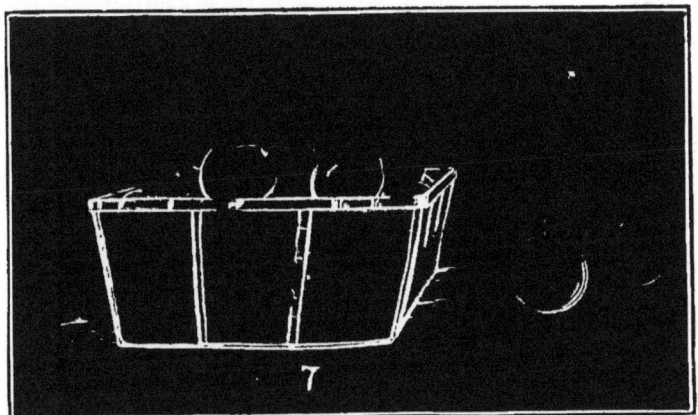

Fig. 7 represents a blackboard drawing of a fruit basket drawn below and at the left of the eye, and filled with peaches. Fig. 8 is a work-basket drawn below and at the right of the eye.

14. Draw basket 7 below the eye.

15. Draw basket 8 below and at the left of the eye and fill with eggs.

Basket 9 is placed on top of a post. It is above and at the left of the eye. Fig. 10 is a comb-basket attached to a post. It is above and at the right of the eye.

16. Draw basket 9.
17. Draw basket 9 with the right face to the front.
18. Draw basket 9 below and at the left of the eye.
19. Draw basket 10.
20. Draw basket 10 below and at the right of the eye.

LINES.

A line, apparently, may be full of expression. It may express hardness or softness, strength or weakness, the supple, the flexible, the graceful — almost any quality, providing the proper thought guides the pencil. Notwithstanding lines seem to have expression, seem to be pregnant with life and vitality, they, in themselves, really possess none of these, and this fact should be recognized. A line in drawing possesses no expression, no life, no vitality, except as it is imparted and vitalized by the thought behind it.

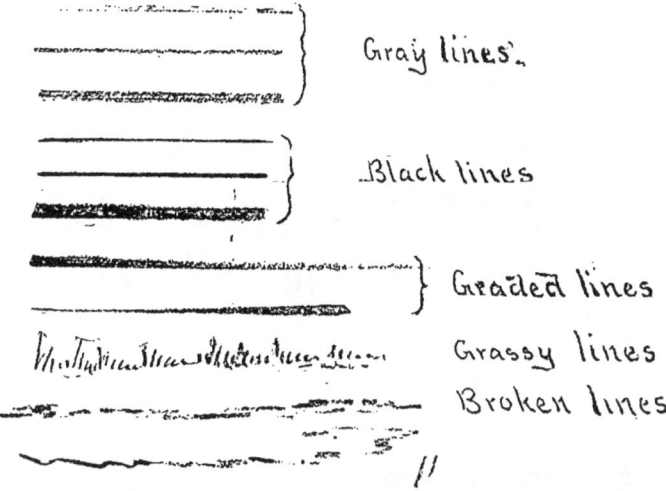

The thought, the idea, is everything, the line nothing; so instead of looking to the line as a source of power, we should look entirely to the thought back of the line.

In general we may divide the lines made with pencil or crayon into :

Gray lines, varying from fine to broad gray.
Black lines, varying from fine to broad black.

Graded lines, lines graded from light to heavy and from heavy to light.

Grassy lines, which are irregular lines in which the vertical predominates.

Broken lines, which are irregular lines to represent irregular surfaces. They may be as variable as the surfaces which they represent.

Every drawing should be represented with a variety of line — with lines varying from light to black, from fine gray to broad gray. The full range of the pencil should be used.

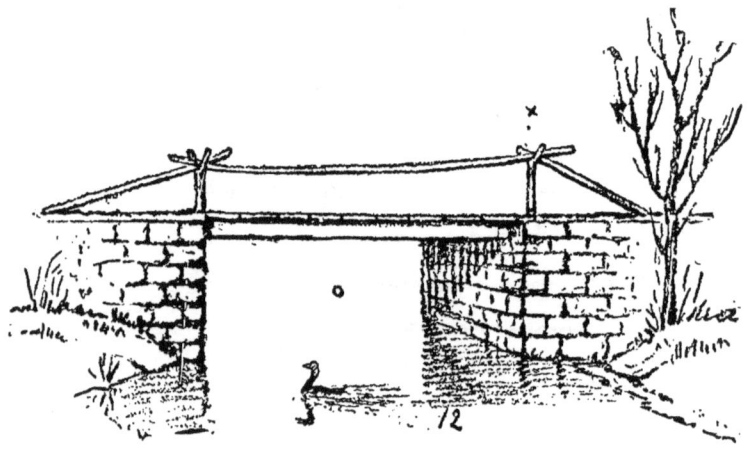

Fig. 12 is a bridge drawn with the top on a level with the eye. All the different kinds of lines are represented in this drawing. In general, the under lines are heavy and black, and the top lines light. Observe how the different surfaces are suggested, the variety of line, and how the material of which the bridge is composed is suggested by the kind of line.

DRILL EXERCISES.

1. Draw Fig. 12.
2. Draw Fig. 12 with the center of vision at X.
3. Draw Fig. 12 with the center of vision at O.

The direction of a line is of more value than its quality. If the direction is wrong, the line is wrong, no matter how nicely it may be drawn.

The direction of the line suggests the direction of the surface; the kind of line, the quality of the surface. For example, a vertical line suggests a *vertical surface;* a horizontal line a *horizontal surface;* an oblique line an *oblique surface;* a curved line a *curved surface,* and a receding line a *receding surface.*

A horizontal straight line indicates a horizontal *flat surface;* a horizontal *grassy* line indicates a horizontal *grassy surface;* a horizontal broken line indicates a horizontal *broken surface,* etc.

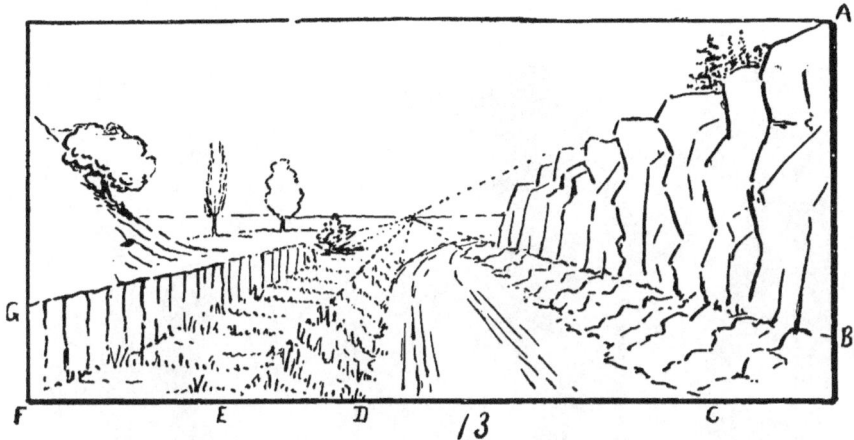

In Fig. 13 the lines between the receding lines, A and B, are broken vertical lines, and they indicate a broken vertical surface. The lines between B and C are broken oblique, and they suggest a broken oblique surface; between C and D, horizontal receding, and they suggest a horizontal receding surface; between D and E, grassy oblique, and they suggest an oblique grassy surface; between E and F, grassy horizontal, and between F and G, vertical and grassy horizontal, and vertical surfaces are suggested.

The horizontal lines at the base of the trees in the distance suggest a horizontal surface.

The oblique line at the base of the tree on the left suggests an oblique surface.

Observe the above ideas on real objects. The representation of ideas will do little good if the ideas themselves cannot be seen outside of the picture in which they are represented.

4. Draw Fig. 13.

5. Draw the fence in Fig. 13, and represent it as leaning to the right, as if partly blown over.

6. Represent the fence as leaning to the left.

7. Represent the cliff as composed of *oblique* broken lines.

Modifying and Changing Objects.

Most objects may be modified, without changing their general form, in three ways: (1) By changing their position in regard to the eye. (2) By changing the material of which they are composed. (3) By arranging the details differently.

Figs. 14-22 represent nine shanties alike in form, but differing in *position*, *material*, and *details*. These shanties correspond to the nine positions of the box, Figs. 2-10, Chapter I.

The center of vision may be found in each drawing, by the continuation of two or more receding lines. It is marked by an X in each drawing. The center of vision is always in the horizon line.

Shanty 14 represents a blackboard drawing of a hen-house. It is drawn at the left of the eye. Observe that it is made of rough boards arranged horizontally.

DRILL EXERCISES.

1. Draw Fig. 14.
2. Draw Fig. 14 directly in front of the eye. Place two trees at the left of it.

Fig. 15 is a pen drawing of a fisherman's shanty, drawn at the right of the eye. Observe that the boards are arranged vertically.

3. Draw Fig. 15.
4. Draw Fig. 15 at the left of the eye.
5. Draw Fig. 15 in front of the eye, and arrange the details according to your own idea.

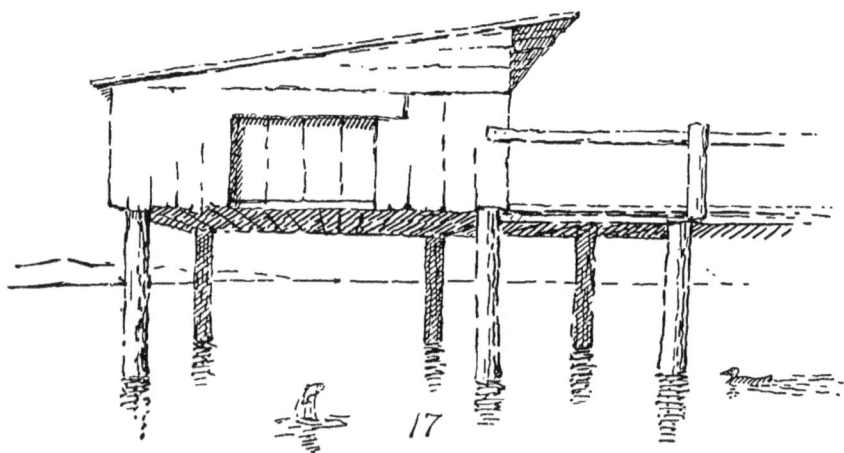

AUGSBURG'S DRAWING.

Fig. 16 is a pen drawing of a shed, drawn directly in front of the eye. The shed has a thatched roof. The level of the eye corresponds with the top of the board fence.

6. Draw Fig. 16.
7. Draw Fig. 16 at the left of the eye. Board up the left and back faces.

Fig. 17 is a pen drawing of a boat-house, drawn above the level of the eye.

8. Draw Fig. 17.
9. Draw Fig. 17 at the left of the eye and resting on the ground.

Fig. 18 is a wash drawing of the shanty turned into a dwelling-house. It is above and at the left of the eye.

19

20

10. Draw Fig. 18.
11. Draw Fig. 18 as a shed similar to Fig. 16.

Fig. 19 represents a brick powder-house, drawn above and at the right of the eye.

12. Draw Fig. 19.
13. Draw Fig. 19 above and at the left of the eye.

Fig. 20 is a pencil-drawing of a hermit's cabin, drawn below the eye. It is covered with shingles both on top and the sides.

14. Draw Fig. 20.
15. Draw Fig. 20 below and at the right of the eye. Place a different landscape around it.
16. Draw Fig. 20 at the left of the eye.

Fig. 21 is a miner's cabin, drawn below and at the left of the eye.

If the center of vision is changed, the horizon line must be changed also.

17. Draw Fig. 21.
18. Draw Fig. 21 at the left of the eye.

Fig. 22 is a pencil-drawing of a summer kitchen, drawn below and at the right of the eye.

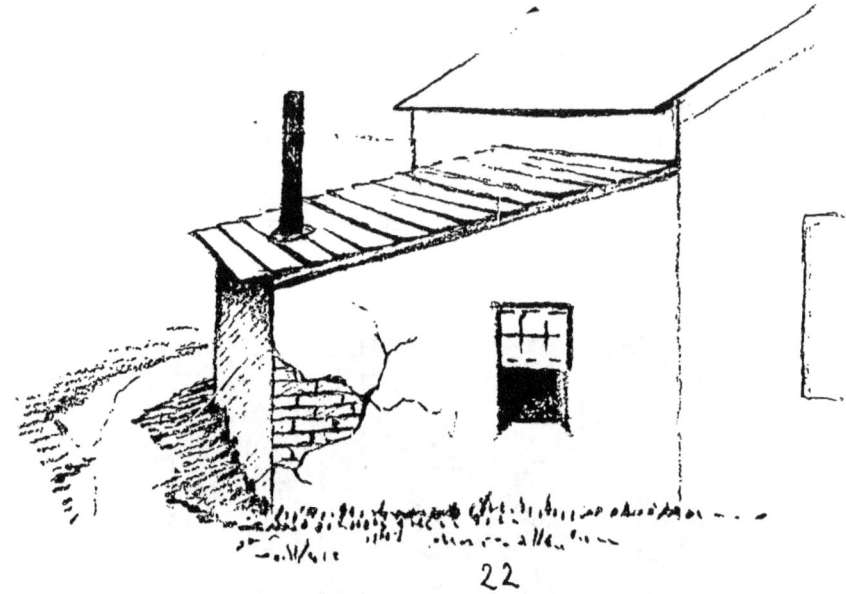

19. Draw Fig. 22. Introduce four trees beyond the house.
20. Draw Fig. 22 at the right of the eye.

The above shanties may be further modified: (1) By turning them so the front or back face will be toward you. (2) By placing on them a gable roof. (3) By changing them so as to conform to some building in your vicinity.

CHAPTER V.

OBLIQUE DRAWING.

Thus far the center of vision has been used as an aid in learning how to represent receding surfaces and to give a definite point to which the receding lines are drawn. But now we have advanced far enough to dispense with the aid of this point, and to depend on the unaided eye in drawing the surfaces. Our guide will be: *Does the drawing appear right? If it appears right we are to take it for granted that it is right, for to us this will be true until our ideal becomes more perfect.*

The picture plane is the plane on which the picture is drawn, as the paper or blackboard. It is a *real* plane.

The ground plane is an *imaginary* plane beginning at the *ground line*, G L, Fig. 1, and reaching out to the horizon line, E L (level of the eye). It is at right angles with the picture plane.

In the drawing, Fig. 1, there are two boxes, A and B. Box A is such as we have been drawing, and contains vertical, horizontal, and horizontal receding lines, and the receding lines converge to the center of vision.

Box B is represented with vertical and receding lines, and the receding lines converge to vanishing points in the horizon line, right and left of the center of vision.

These receding lines that converge in the horizon line outside of the center of vision are called *oblique horizontal receding lines*. Oblique because they are at an oblique angle with the picture plane; horizontal because parallel with the ground plane; and receding because they pass from you — recede.

Receding lines 1, 2 and 3 are horizontal receding lines, and receding lines 4, 5, 6, 7, 8, and 9 are oblique horizontal receding.

It is not practicable or desirable to use these vanishing points in ordinary drawing, for the following reasons:

(1) Because one of these points is and usually both are outside of the paper on which the drawing is made, and thus too

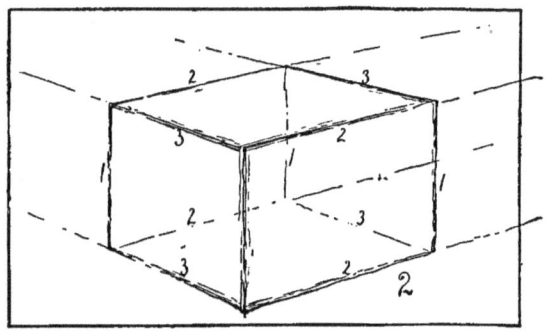

far away. (2) Their use draws the attention from the object and lessens the range of the judgment. (3) . Their use is not practical, satisfactory or necessary.

But while the above is true, a knowledge of these points is of great aid to the judgment in determining the direction of lines and surfaces.

Box A is said to be drawn in *parallel perspective* and Box B in *angular perspective*.

Lines and Models.— Place before you a common pasteboard box in the position of Fig. 2 and observe the three sets of lines 1, 1, 1, 1; 2, 2, 2, 2; 3, 3, 3, 3. The first set are vertical and parallel. The sets marked 2, 2, 2, 2, and 3, 3, 3, 3, are receding, and consequently converge slightly, *but in the drawing they should not appear to converge, but should appear parallel — they should appear natural*.

Draw all objects with *light lines* and then finish with heavier. Draw the receding lines longer than the edge of the object so as to judge more accurately of their correctness.

Use the model to verify, to correct and to perfect the mind image. A common pasteboard box is an excellent model.

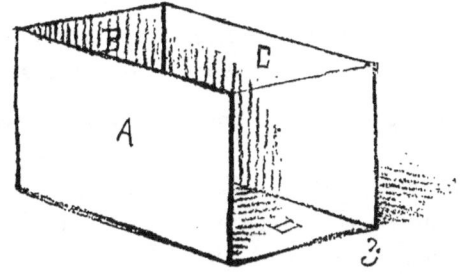

Shading.— Shading may be used in connection with this work providing it is used as a means of expression — as a means of bringing out the idea and making it plain. It is the office of shading to help the weak — the weak side of the idea. In these problems *those faces may be regarded as weak that are represented by less than four lines*. The surface on which the object rests, having no lines to represent it, may be regarded as weak.

In Fig. 3, face A is represented by four lines, therefore needs no shade to strengthen it. Face B is represented by only two lines, hence is regarded as weak and is shaded. Faces C and D are weak where they are covered by face A, hence are strengthened with shade lines at these points. This is merely suggestive *and is not intended to limit the use of shade on strong faces, if there is reason to place it there*.

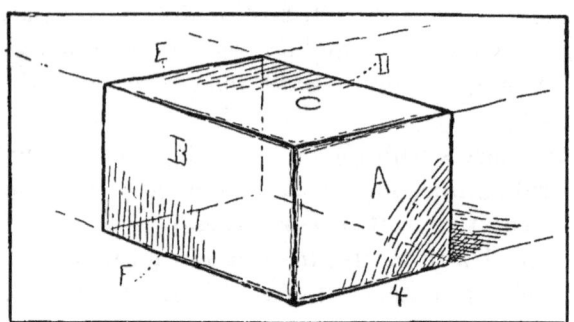

Curved faces are always weak, having only one and never more than two lines to indicate the curvature, hence they may be shaded.

NOTE.— See the chapter on Wash Drawing in Book III. for full directions in shading.

Fig. 4 is a box with the faces marked with letters. Draw this box and remove the faces as given in the exercises below. Use for a model a common pasteboard box.

DRILL EXERCISES.

1. Remove faces A, C and E.
2. Remove faces A, B and E.
3. Remove faces A and D.
4. Remove faces A and F.

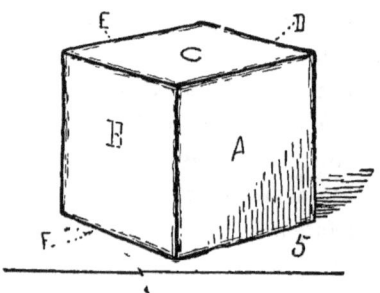

5. Remove faces B, C and D.
6. Remove faces B and F.
7. Remove faces B and E.
8. Remove faces C and D.

Use for models four cubical blocks. Four crayon boxes are excellent models for general use.

Fig. 5 is a small cube. Add similar cubes to the faces as follows:

9. Add to face C a similar cube.
10. Add to faces B and D similar cubes.
11. Add to faces A and B similar cubes.
12. Add to faces A, C and E similar cubes.
13. Add a similar cube to each face.
14. Place cubes one block from faces A and B.
15. Place cubes one block from faces D and E.

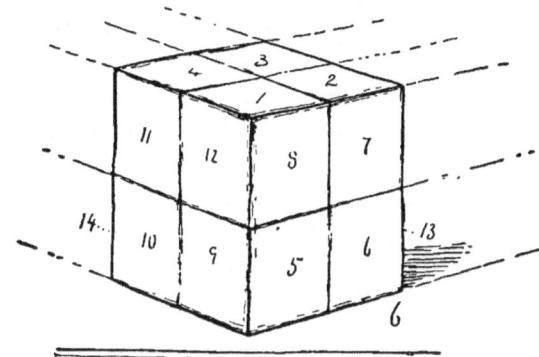

Fig. 6 is a large cube composed of eight smaller ones. Add similar cubes to the small ones as follows:

16. Add cubes to faces 3, 6 and 10.
17. Add cubes to faces 1, 5 and 9.
18. Add cubes to faces 4, 13 and 14.
19. Add cubes to faces 2, 7 and 12.

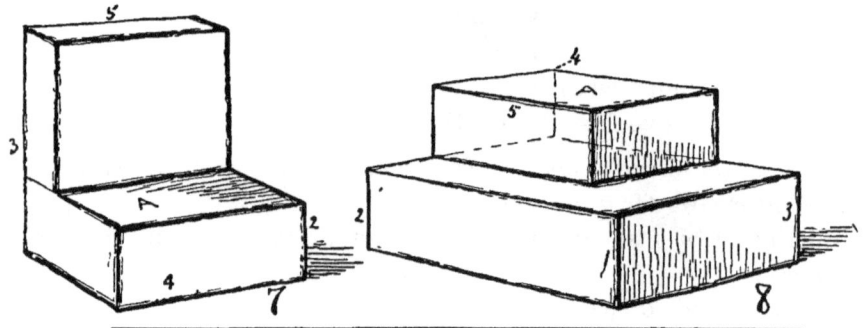

20. Remove cube 1.
21. Remove cubes 3 and 6.
22. Remove cubes 4 and 5.

Figs. 7 and 8 are two very serviceable models made by nailing or gluing two blocks together. Fig. 7 is L shaped. Fig. 8 is made by placing a smaller block on a larger, so that one corner and two sides are even. These blocks are the same as blocks 11 and 12 in Chapter III. These models are to be held in the hand when drawing at the blackboard, or placed on the seat when drawing on the tablets.

Do not aim at exactness of proportion, but rather to gain the principle and to represent the block in the position called for. *Do not require these problems to be drawn without a model for the pupil to look at.*

23. Draw block 7.
24. Draw block 7 with edge 3 toward you.
25. Draw block 7 with edge 2 toward you.
26. Draw block 7 with edge 4 vertical and toward you.
27. Draw block 7 with edge 5 vertical and toward you.
28. Draw block 8.
29. Draw block 8 with edge 2 toward you.

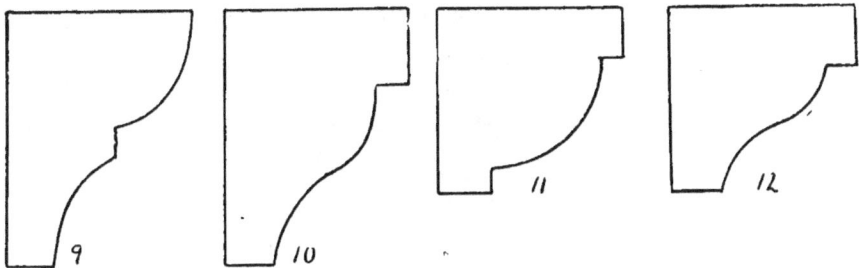

30. Draw block 8 with face A down and edge 4 toward you.
31. Draw block 8 with edge 5 vertical and toward you.
32. Draw block 8 with edge 1 toward you and face A down.

Figs. 9–12 represent pieces of common moulding such as are used by most carpenters and builders. These pieces of moulding make excellent models for drill purpose. They should be cut about one inch long. The moulding need not necessarily be exactly like Figs. 9, 10, 11 and 12, but should be as simple. The models are used in the same manner as blocks 7 and 8.

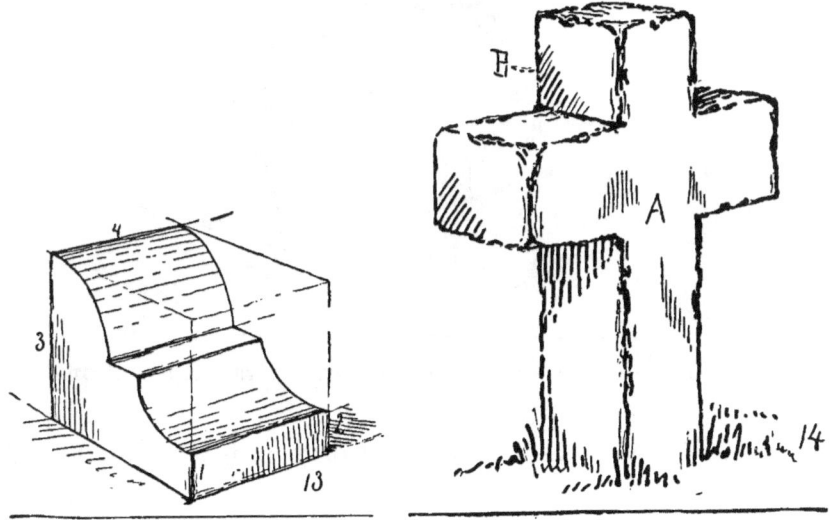

Fig. 13 shows model 9 drawn in one position.

33. Draw moulding 9 in the position of Fig. 13.
34. Draw the same with edge 3 toward you.
35. Draw the same with edge 4 vertical and toward you.

36. Draw Fig. 14.
37. Draw Fig. 14 lying on face A.
38. Draw the cross lying on face B.
39. Draw the cross resting on the right arm.

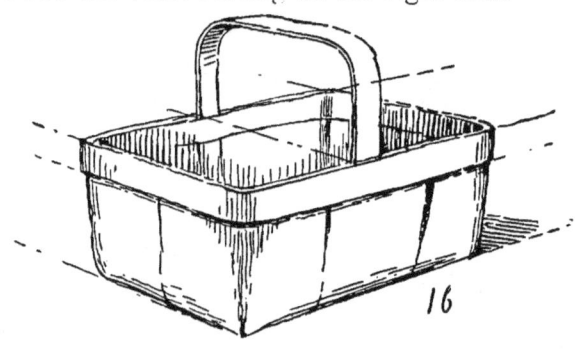

Fig. 15 represents a wooden mallet. Draw it as follows:

40. Draw Fig. 15.
41. Draw the mallet with the handle projecting to the right and toward you.

42. Draw the mallet with the handle projecting to the right and away.
43. Draw the mallet with the handle projecting upward.
44. Draw Fig. 16.
45. Draw the basket with the long part to the left and away.

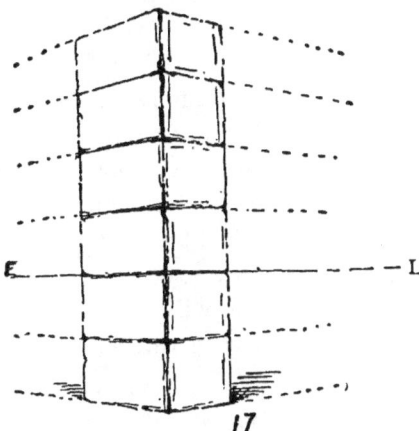

When the object is both below and above the level of the eye, as Figs. 17 and 18, then it is well to locate the level of the eye in order to judge more accurately of the slant of the receding lines.

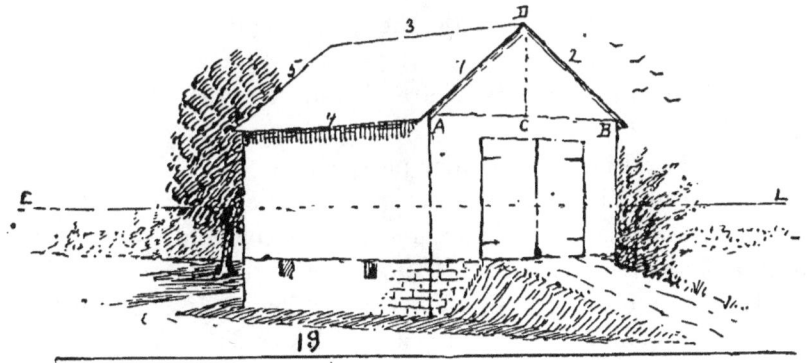

Fig. 17 represents several boxes piled one above the other. Observe (1) that the receding lines above the level of the eye *slant downward*. (2) That the receding lines below the level of the eye *slant upward*. (3) That the receding lines on a level with the eye are horizontal. The eye level determines the slant of the lines. The further the receding lines above or below the level of the eye the more they slant.

In Fig. 18 observe that the receding lines above and below the eye level obey this law the same as in the boxes. They slant downward and upward to the level of the eye.

Fig. 18, and all similar buildings, may be drawn as follows: (1) Draw the body part of the building the same as the box. (2) To put the roof on, bisect A B as at C and from this point erect a vertical line as high as you wish the apex D. (3) Draw lines 1 and 2. (4) Draw line 3 which will slant to the eye level, and draw line 5 practically parallel with line 1.

NOTE.— It is an excellent drill exercise to place a gable roof on each one of the shanties represented in Chapter IV. and to draw both the baskets and shanties in oblique perspective.

DRILL EXERCISE.

46. Draw Fig. 18.

47. Draw the barn with the gable end to the left and toward you.

The following exercises are based on the drawings in Chapter IV.

48. Draw Fig. 1 in angular perspective.

49. Draw Fig. 2 in angular perspective. Fig. 4. Fig. 7.

50. Draw shanty 14 in angular perspective and place a gable roof on it similar to the roof of the barn in Fig. 18.

51. Do the same with shanty 15. Shanty 16. Shanty 17. Shanty 18. Shanty 19. Shanty 20. Shanty 21.

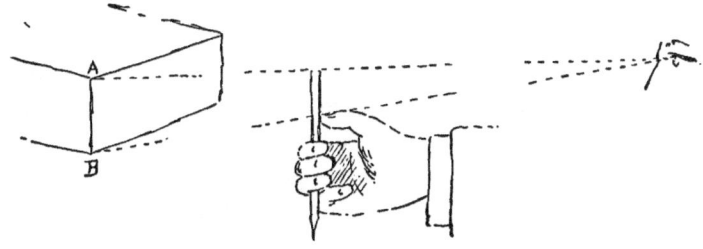

CHAPTER VI.

Exact Drawing.

The Aim in this chapter is to show a method of drawing square-cornered objects exactly as they appear to the eye in form and proportion.

Thus far in our drawing, exactness in form and proportion has not been required. We have been using the object as an idea to be reproduced unhampered by the annoyance arising from exactness. The mind being relieved from these lesser requirements had more freedom to acquire the higher and more important element — PRINCIPLE.

The method now to be presented may be used for the drawing of *all square-cornered objects*. But it must be remembered that method should not, as is too often the case, be taken for the understanding that enables one to draw. Method at the most is but an *orderly way of doing*. Simply knowing the method will not enable one to draw, any more than a mere knowledge of notes will enable one to sing. A method is a tool to work with, the same as the pencil, only less material: it is the road, but not the destination.

The object should be placed at least three times its height away. It may be further than this, but if nearer it may appear distorted.

83

Measuring.— Procure a box (a common crayon box is an excellent model) and place it before you as in Fig. 2. To measure the edge A B, hold your pencil at easy arm's length away; close one eye; let the upper end of the pencil correspond in height with corner A on the box, and with your thumb mark corner B as in Fig. 1. This does not measure the real length of line 1, but simply gives a unit with which to compare other lines. For example: you measure line 1 and compare it with the length of line 2 to see which is the longer. In order to learn how to thus measure, make the following measurements:

1. Compare the length of line 1 with the length of line 2. Which is the longer?
2. Compare the length of line 1 with the length of line 3.
3. Which is the longer, line 2 or line 3?
4. Which is the longer, line 1 or the horizontal distance between lines 1 and 2?

NOTE.— This measuring with the pencil is done by simply turning the hand on the wrist. Care must be taken when making this and all similar comparisons *not to let the pencil slant or recede in the direction of the receding surface.* The pencil must be kept at right angles with the arm at all times when measuring. This is the most important point in measuring and must be observed.

5. Which is longer, the length of line 1 or the horizontal distance between lines 2 and 3?
6. Which is the longer, the distance between lines 1 and 2 or between 1 and 3?
7. Which is the longer, the distance between lines 2 and 3 or between points B and G?

Drawing the Box.— The general process of drawing box shaped objects is as follows:

(1) Draw the nearest vertical line.
(2) Find the remaining vertical lines.

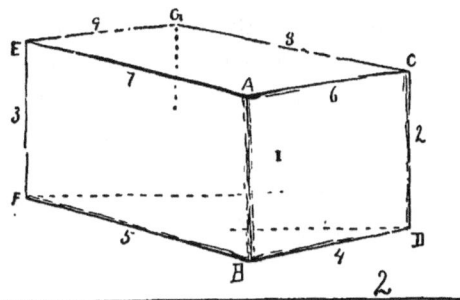

(3) Find the corners.
(4) Finish.

Let us take this up step by step.

First Step: Draw the nearest vertical line. Place the box in position as in Fig. 2. Draw the nearest vertical line any length you wish. This line, when drawn, becomes the unit of measure for all the other lines *in the drawing.* The length of this line determines the size of the box. If the line is drawn long, the box will be large; if short, small. The length of this drawn line has nothing to do with the real length of the edge it represents.

Second Step: Find the remaining vertical lines. Find the position of vertical line 2, by comparing the length of line 1 with the horizontal distance between lines 1 and 2, and making the same comparison in your drawing. Find line 3 in the same manner. Draw lines 2 and 3 lightly and of indefinite length.

Third Step: Find the corners. To find corner D in the drawing pass your pencil horizontally through corner D on the box and note where your pencil crosses edge 1 — that is, how far above corner B or below corner A it crosses; mark this point in your drawing on line 1 and from this point draw a light horizontal line. Where this line crosses line 2 it will mark corner D. Find corner F in the same manner and draw lines 4 or 5.

Fourth Step: Finish. Draw lines 6 and 9 parallel with line

4, and lines 7 and 8 parallel with line 5, in the same manner as in Chapter V. You can prove whether you have corner G in the right place by passing your pencil vertically through corner G and noting where it crosses line 7 or 6, and then making a similar comparison in your drawing. *Any unknown point may be found by finding how far to the right or left and how far above or below it is of a given point in your drawing.* For practice draw boxes placed as follows:

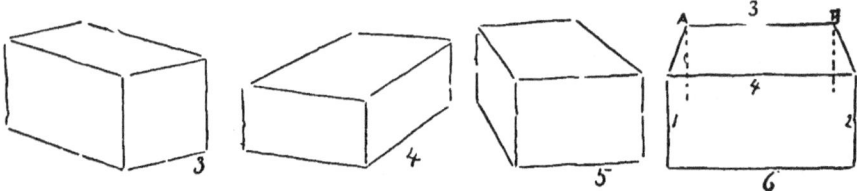

8. Place a box in the position of Fig. 3 and draw it.
9. Place a box in the position of Fig. 4 and draw it.
10. Place a box in the position of Fig. 5 and draw it.
11. Place a box in the position of Fig. 6 and draw it.

NOTE.—In this position lines 1 and 2 will be the same length and lines 3, 4 and 5 will be horizontal. Line 3 is found by comparing the length of line 1 with the vertical distance between lines 3 and 4 and making the same comparison in the drawing. Corners A and B may be found by passing the pencil vertically through corners A and B on the model and noting where it crosses line 4. Marking these points on line 4 in the drawing and from them drawing light vertical lines will mark corners A and B.

Perceptive and Conceptive Drawing.— The method used when drawing a percept, that is, in drawing the object exactly as it appears to the eye, is not the same as when drawing a concept of the object, or when the object is not before the eye. For example, if Fig. 6, an object below the level of the eye, is to be drawn exactly as it appears to the eye, it would not be practicable to use the center of vision. Why? Because the effort of finding the exact location of this point would be as much trouble as drawing the object. The center of vision is a point that cannot be seen. The lines and corners on the box which this point is to aid in finding, can be seen; hence, when the object is before you, it is easier to find these points and lines without the aid of the center of vision.

But if Fig. 6 is to be drawn below the level of the eye from the concept or thought alone, then as all points and lines are invisible, the center of vision may be used very effectively. The same may be said of the horizon line, vanishing points, and similar devices. *So, generally speaking, the devices used in drawing an object perceptively are not practicable when drawing an object conceptively.*

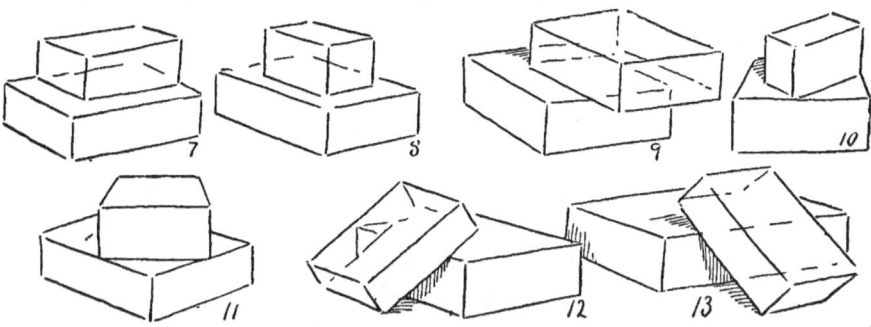

12. Place two boxes in the position of Fig. 7 and draw them. (The first box drawn becomes the unit of measure for the other box.)

13. Place boxes in the position of Fig. 8 and draw them.
14. Place boxes in the position of Fig. 9 and draw them.
15. Place boxes in the position of Fig. 10 and draw them.
16. Place boxes in the position of Fig. 11 and draw them.
17. Place boxes in the position of Fig. 12 and draw them.
18. Place boxes in the position of Fig. 13 and draw them.

Procure for a model a lunch box similar to Fig. 14. Draw it as follows:

19. Place the lunch box in the position of Fig. 4 and draw it.

20. Place the lunch box in the position of Fig. 5 and draw it.

Other positions are: resting on its side, end, with the cover removed, and leaning against something.

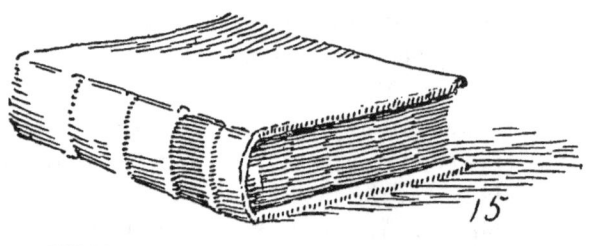

Procure a thick and well worn book, place it in the following positions and draw it:

21. Draw the book in the position of Fig. 4.
22. Draw the book in the position of Fig. 5.
23. Draw the book in the position of Fig. 6.
24. Draw the book open.
25. Draw the book partly open.

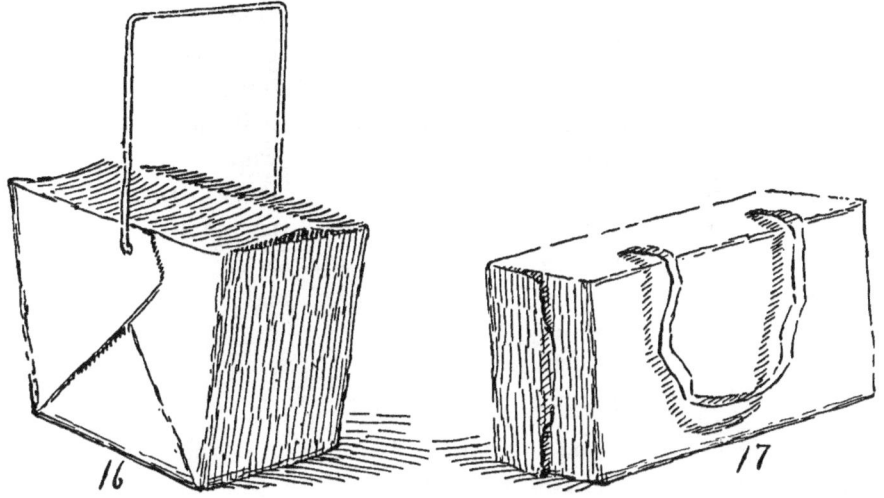

Procure for a model a pickle or oyster box, Fig. 16, and a plain candy box, Fig. 17, and draw them as follows:

26. Place the pickle box in the position of Fig. 4 and draw it.
27. Place the candy box in the position of Fig. 5 and draw it.
28. Place the two boxes together in a pleasing position and draw them.

AUGSBURG'S DRAWING.

The following list of square-cornered objects will be found convenient to suggest what to draw, both for practice and for use in the class-room:

boxes	packages	raft	boat-house
book	blocks	punt	block-house
chair	stones	scow	stockade
chest	eraser	wood-pile	steps
trunk	dishes	cage	fireplace
table	oil-stone	safe	tower
baskets	trough	coffee-mill	hall
bookcase	sign	house	wall
trap	beehive	barn	fence corner
wagon	bureau	shed	bridge
brick	door	shanty	cab
bar of soap	window	cabin	car
stool	chimney	tent	cart
bench	wharf	room	post
oil-can	dock	bird-house	tunnel

In general, plain and simple objects, crudely formed objects, old and broken objects, and natural objects are preferable. New

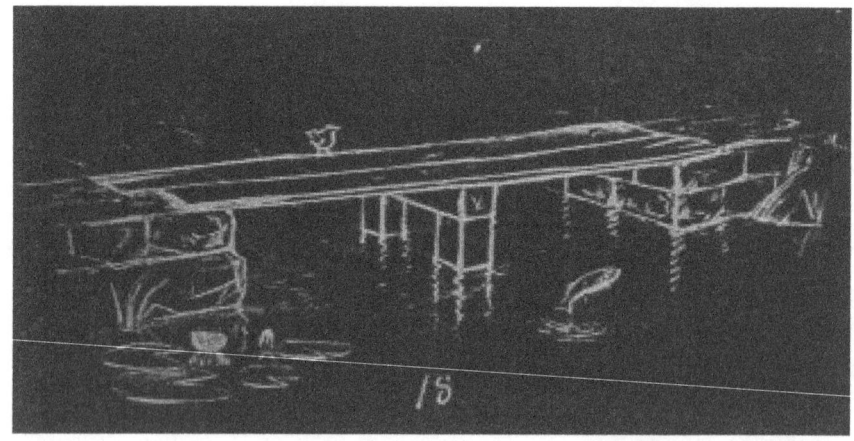

AUGSBURG'S DRAWING.

objects, delicately formed and finished objects, complicated objects, and decorated objects are not suitable.

There are many objects all about us suitable for drawing if we can see and recognize them, but they are so often confused with other objects that they fail of recognition. In drawing, we have both the right and the power to choose or reject at pleasure. In Fig. 18 there were any number of objects beyond the foot-bridge — the bank of the stream, lily pads, bulrushes, and trees — but as the foot-bridge was the only part wanted, the remaining parts and details were rejected. We should not introduce more into our drawing than is necessary to complete the idea.

To draw houses proceed the same as if the object were a box. Fig. 19 may be drawn as follows: (1) Draw A B the nearest vertical line. (2) Find lines 1 and 2 and locate corners D and C, E and F. (3) Bisect A E and locate the apex G. (4) Locate the apex H. Bear in mind that the receding lines above the level of the eye slant downward.

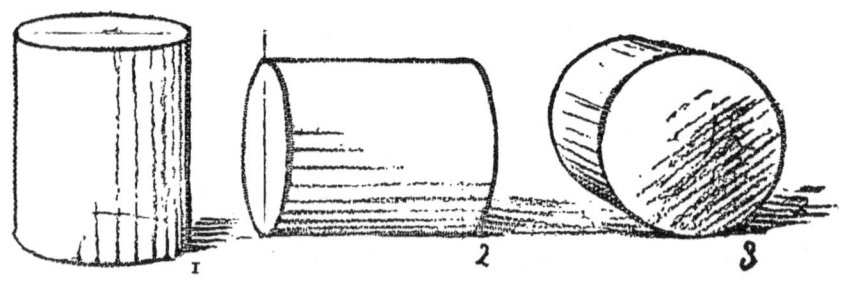

CHAPTER VII.

THE CYLINDER.

The cylinder is the type form for objects containing curved lines and surfaces.

For convenience, the study of the cylinder is divided into *the vertical cylinder*, Fig. 1; *the horizontal cylinder*, Fig. 2; *the horizontal-receding cylinder*, Fig. 3, corresponding to the vertical, horizontal, and horizontal-receding lines.

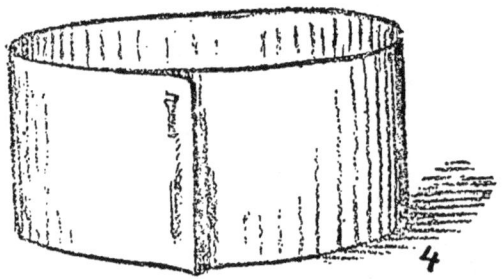

THE VERTICAL CYLINDER.

Models.— Use for a model a strip of rather stiff paper, 1½ x 9 inches, bent round, with the ends pinned or pasted, as in Fig. 4. A common fruit can, baking-powder can, and a plain cylindrical glass tumbler, all make excellent models. Use several models. Often we can see in one model what we fail to see in another.

Use both perceptive and conceptive knowledge in the study of the cylinder. Your general knowledge of the cylinder, and the knowledge derived from the model, should go hand in hand. E L (eye level) is the horizon line that marks the level of the eye.

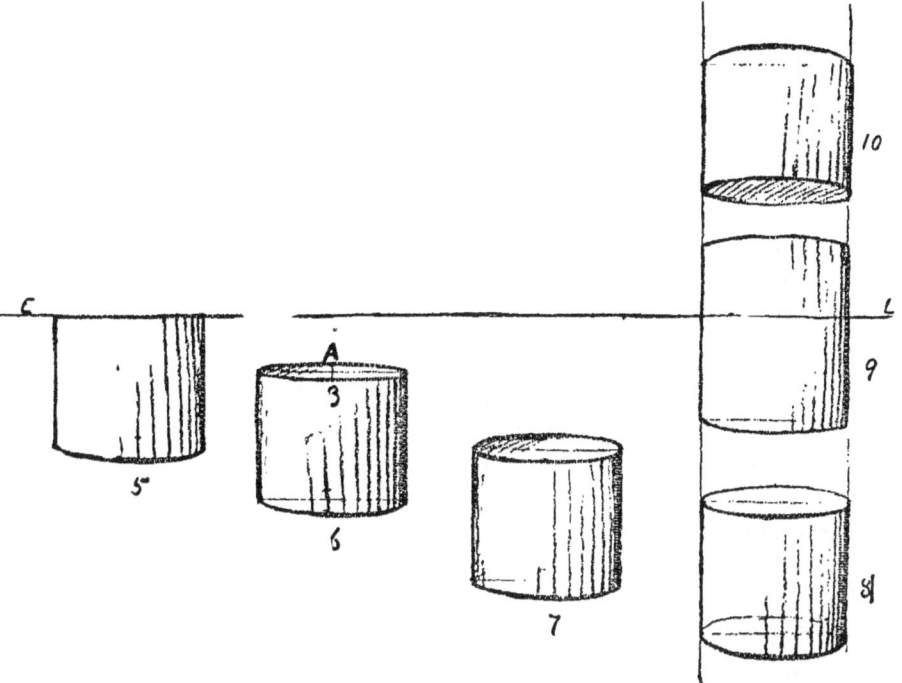

The Vertical Cylinder.— Hold the model in your hand at easy arm's length away, so that the top is on a level with your eye, as in Fig. 5. Observe: (1) That the top of the cylinder is represented by a horizontal line. (2) That the bottom curves downward. This can be seen very clearly with a glass tumbler for a model. A pencil placed across the top, and then held across the bottom, will also help to show the curvature.

Hold the cylinder in the position of Fig. 7, and observe: (1) That the top is an ellipse. (2) That the bottom curves downward.

Hold the cylinder in the position of Fig. 5, then in the position of Fig. 6, then of Fig. 7 and Fig. 8, and observe: (1) That the top appears wider in each succeeding position; *that the farther it is placed below the level of the eye, the wider it appears;* (2) That the farther it is placed below the eye, the more the bottom appears to curve downward.

Hold the cylinder below the eye in the position of Fig. 8, and then above the eye, in the position of Fig. 10, and observe that when the cylinder is below the eye the top can be seen, and when above the eye the bottom can be seen.

Hold the cylinder on a level with the eye as in Fig. 9, and observe: (1) That neither the top nor bottom can be seen. (2) That the top curves upward and the bottom downward.

Hold a cylinder in the position of Fig. 6, and measure the width A B with the lead pencil; measure the same width in the positions 7 and 8, and note how they vary.

With the above data as an aid, draw the vertical cylinder in the following positions:

1. Draw a vertical cylinder below the eye.
2. Draw a vertical cylinder below the eye and remove the top face.

NOTE.— *When drawing a vertical cylinder, or cylinders, in any position, it is necessary to draw both ends entire. It is often necessary to draw the whole in order to represent the part correctly.*

3. Draw a vertical cylinder with the top on a level with the eye.
4. Draw a vertical cylinder above the eye.
5. Draw a vertical cylinder with the middle on a level with the eye.

6. Draw a vertical cylinder below the eye. Place a ball on top of it, an apple in front, and an apple on each side.

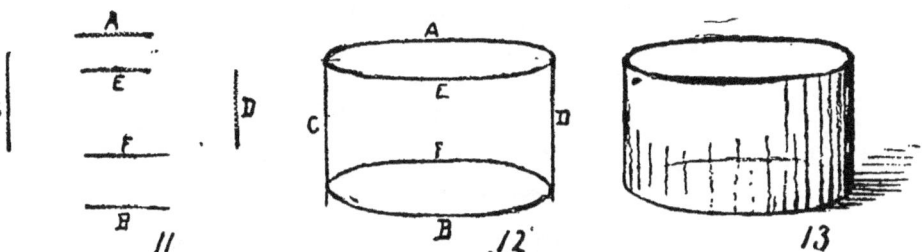

Problems 1–6 were drawn without regard to the exact proportion. The aim was simply to draw *a cylinder in a given position.* Now we will learn to draw a cylinder in exact proportion, as it appears to the eye.

The following is a simple and effective formula, not only for drawing the cylinder, but for nearly all objects:
1. Take the length, or height.
2. Find the width.
3. Find the prominent points.
4. Finish.

Let us do this more in detail. (1) Place the cylinder before you, as in Fig. 13. (2) Take the height A B, Fig. 11. Any height may be taken, as the size of the drawing has little to do with the size of the object. *The size of the drawing is usually adapted to the size of the space it is to occupy on the paper.* (3) Find the width C D by measuring with your pencil and comparing with the length A B. *(See Measuring, Chapter VI.)* (4) Find prominent points. There is only one to find — the width of the top A E. Find this by comparing it with the distance A E, and draw the top, Fig. 12. (5) The bottom is farther below the eye than the top, hence it will be a trifle wider. Make B F a little wider than E A, and draw the bottom F B, Fig. 12. It is

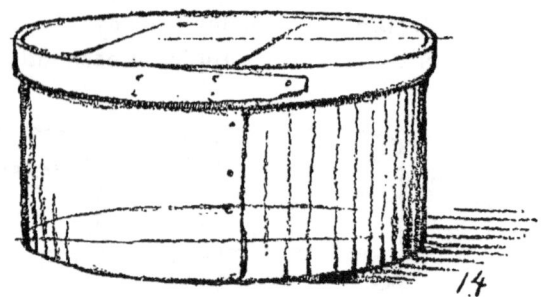

necessary to draw the entire bottom in order to get correctly the line which does show. (6) Finish as Fig. 13.

Procure a cylindrical box, a rough one is preferable, such as Fig. 14, or similar box. Size has little to do with the choice, as the principle is the same for all sizes. Place the cylinder in the following positions, and draw it. *Draw from a real model. Do not use Fig. 14 as a model*:

7. Place the cylindrical box below the level of the eye, and draw it. (Fig. 14.)
8. Place the box with the top on a level with the eye, and draw it. (Fig. 5.)
9. Place the box with the bottom on a level with the eye, and draw it.
10. Place the box above the level of the eye and draw it.
11. Place the box with the middle on the level with the eye and draw it. (Fig. 9.)

Procure for a model a hat similar to Fig. 15, and draw it in various positions as suggested below. Do not skip from one object to another, but choose a hat and draw it in various positions until the principle is thoroughly learned. Use the formula given above. One object well learned is the key to the representation of all similar objects, and indirectly to all objects.

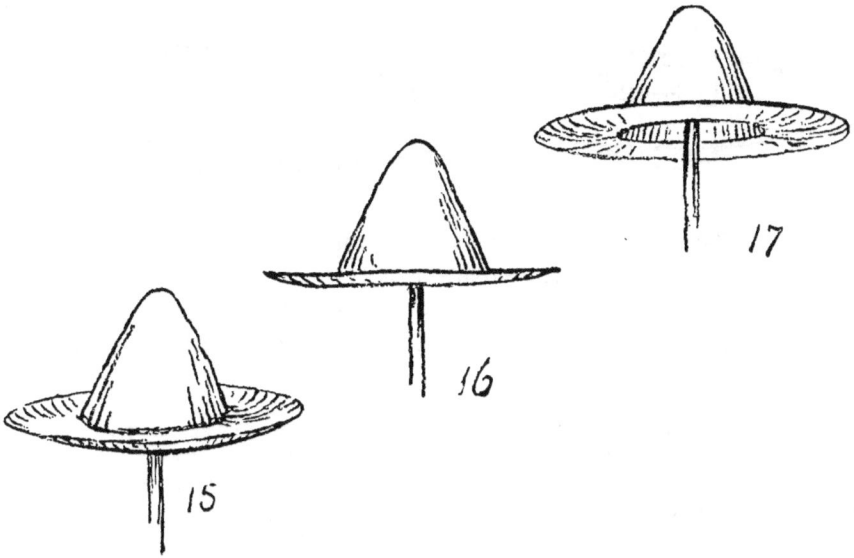

The hats in Figs. 15–19 are balanced on the end of a broom-handle, cane or stick, where they may be seen to better advantage.

12. Place a hat in the position of Fig. 15 and draw it.
13. Place a hat in the position of Fig. 16 and draw it.
14. Place a hat in the position of Fig. 17 and draw it.
15. Place a hat in the position of Fig. 18 and draw it.

 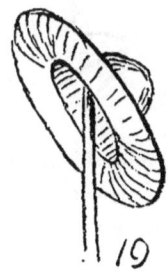

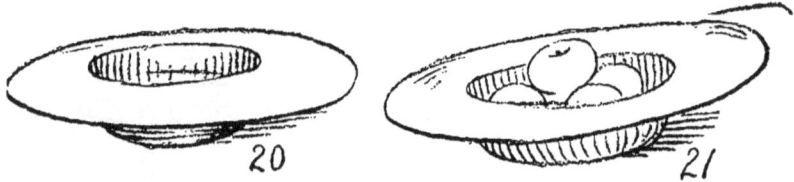

16. Place a hat in the position of Fig. 19 and draw it.
17. Place a hat in the position of Fig. 20 and draw it.
18. Place a hat in the position of Fig. 21 and draw it.
19. Draw a hat in the position of Fig. 20 and fill it with apples.

NOTE.— Any kind of a hat or cap may be drawn in these various positions. Pupils should be encouraged to place their own hat or cap in several of these positions and a drawing be made from each. Let the formula given above be used with each drawing.

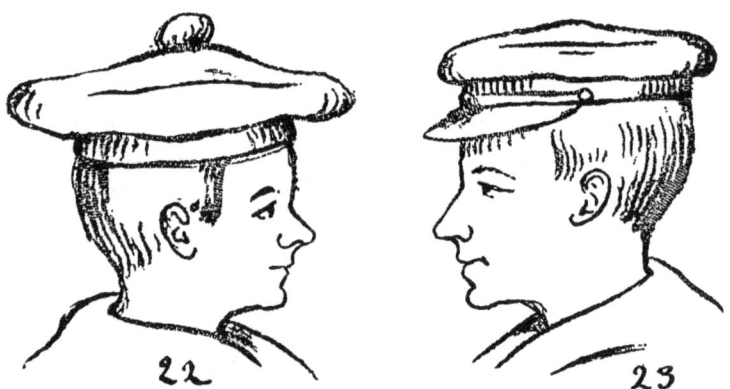

A hat or cap placed on the head of a pupil is not only an excellent but a very interesting model.

Place a cap similar to Fig. 22 or 23 in the position of Fig. 15 and draw it. In the position of Fig. 16. Fig. 17. Fig. 18. Fig. 19. Fig. 20. Fig. 21.

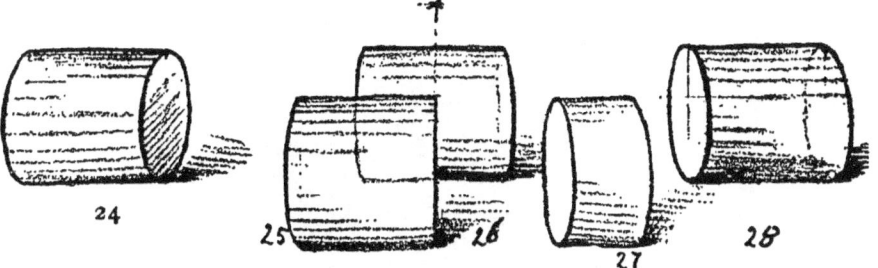

The Horizontal Cylinder.

The horizontal cylinder is the same to the right and left that the vertical cylinder is up and down.

Hold the model at the left of the eye, as in Fig. 24, and observe: (1) That you can see the right face, that it is elliptical in shape, and that the farther to the left it is moved the wider this face appears; (2) that the left face (which can not be seen except in a glass model) is wider than the right face.

Hold the cylinder in the positions of Fig. 27, and observe: (1) That the left face shows that it is elliptical in shape, and appears wider the farther to the right it is moved; (2) that the right face can not be seen but in the drawing is drawn wider than the left face.

Move the cylinder from left to right and from right to left several times and observe: (1) That when the cylinder is at the left of the eye the right face is seen, and when at the right of the eye the left face is seen; (2) when below, above, or in front of the eye neither face can be seen, as shown in Fig. 26; (3) when either face is in line with the eye, as in Fig. 25, the end is represented by a vertical line; (4) that the point opposite the eye (center of vision) determines the drawing of the horizontal cylinder.

Observe that when the horizontal cylinder is below and at the left or right of the eye that the longer axis is not vertical, but slants slightly, as shown by A B and C D in Fig. 46.

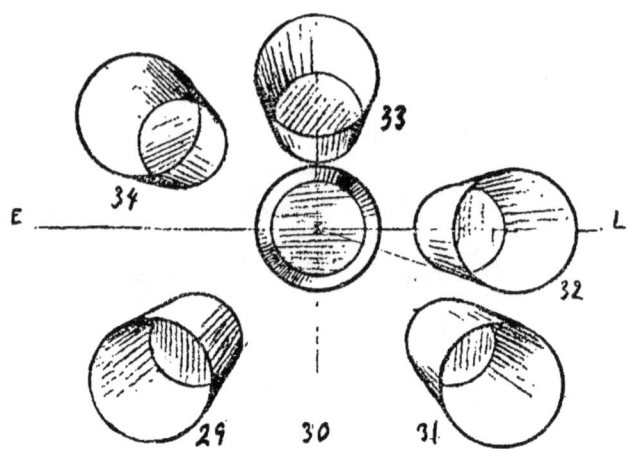

THE HORIZONTAL RECEDING CYLINDER.

Use for a model a common baking powder can. Remove the cover, and hold it in the position of Fig. 30, close one eye, and observe that the farther end of the cylinder is represented by a smaller circle than the nearer end. This is because it is farther away.

Hold the cylinder at the right of the eye as in Fig. 32. In Fig. 30 the end of the cylinder is represented by a circle, but it is evident that as the cylinder is removed to one side of the eye in any direction, that the circle is foreshortened and becomes more and more elliptical. This is true, but within a reasonable distance from the eye the difference is so slight as to become more theoretical than practical, and though the end of Fig. 32 may not be a perfect circle, still because it is more convenient to teach and easier to comprehend, we will speak of it and represent it as one.

Hold the cylinder in the position of Fig. 32 and observe that the circle that represents the further end can be seen partly inside and partly outside the cylinder. Hold the cylinder in the position of Figs. 29, 31, 33 and 34 and observe the appearance of each in comparison with the drawing.

AUGSBURG'S DRAWING. 101

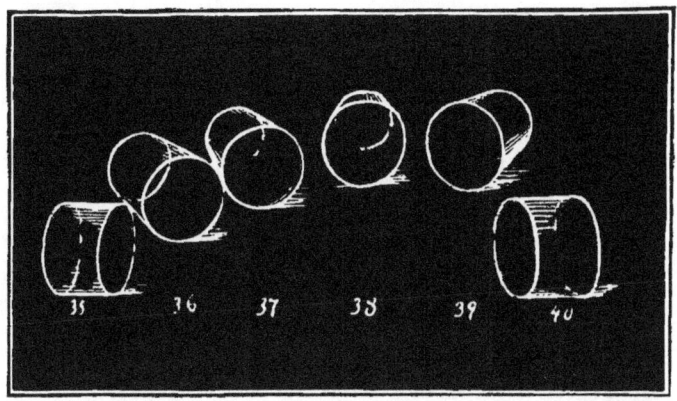

Between the *horizontal* cylinders 35 and 40 and the *horizontal receding* cylinder 38 are oblique horizontal receding cylinders 36, 37 and 39, which are drawn in the same manner as the other cylinders.

Sit at a table or desk and place the model in the position of Fig. 38. In the position of Fig. 36. Fig. 40. Fig. 37. Fig. 39.

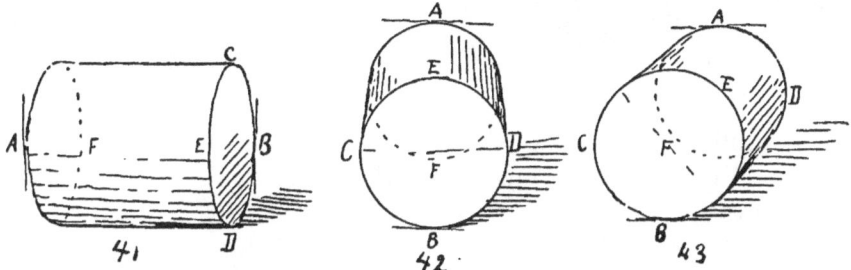

Drawing the Cylinder.— The same method used in drawing the vertical cylinder may be used in drawing cylinders in all positions. This method is similar to that of drawing square-cornered objects in Chapter VI. and is adapted to all kinds of objects. It is as follows:

1. Take the length or height.
2. Find the width.
3. Find prominent points.
4. Block in and finish.

Adapted to Figs. 41, 42 and 43, it is as follows:
1. Take the length or height A B.
2. Find the width C D.
3. The only prominent point to find is E.
4. With these points found, the finishing is very simple.

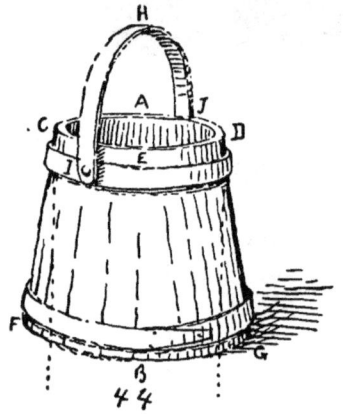
44

45

Applied to objects of almost any kind, for example, the bucket, Fig. 44, or the mug, Fig. 45, the method would be about as follows:
1. Take the height A B.
2. Find the width C D by comparing it with the height.
3. Find prominent points, such as the width of the top A E, the width of the bottom F G; the height or width of the handle H; the points where the handle joins the body as I and J, etc. *These lesser points are taken by the unaided eye. It is comparatively easy to locate a point, if our attention is given to that point*

alone. 4. Finish. After the proportions are found block in the general shape with light lines, then the whole attention can be given to the drawing of the parts.

DRILL EXERCISES.

Procure for a model several cylinders sawed from the limb of a tree similar to Fig. 46, only not so large. If the cylinders contain a knot or other features, so much the better. If these models cannot be procured, a round box such as a baking powder can will do, but it is not so good as a less regular model, such as the limb of a tree with its rough bark and irregular markings. When drawing this object remember that the final decision as to whether the drawing is right or wrong rests with the mind. *Measuring is simply to aid the judgment and is always subordinate to it.*

20. Draw the model as a vertical cylinder similar to Fig. 13.
21. Draw the model in the position of Fig. 35.
22. Draw the model in the position of Fig. 40.

23. Draw the model in the position of Fig. 36.
24. Draw the model in the position of Fig. 39.
25. Draw the model in the position of Fig. 38.
26. Place the model in the position of Fig. 31 and draw it.

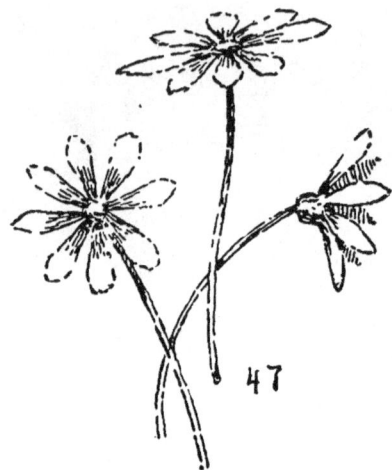

Objects similar to a cylinder are more numerous than those of any other type form. The markings on most fruits, vegetables, and flowers, are based on the principles involved in the cylinder

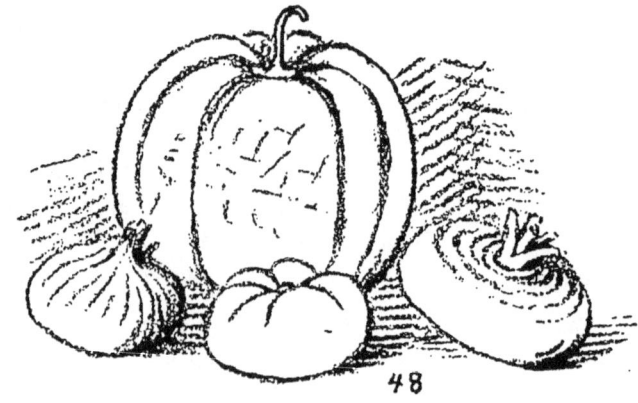

as shown in Figs. 47 and 48, but *the spirit of knowledge can hardly be applied by rule, but by the study of the letter (the rule), we may absorb the spirit which is universal in its application.*

The following is a list of cylindrical shaped objects or objects largely based on the principles involved in the cylinder:

round baskets	keg	can
tub	cheese-box	pitcher
barrel	fig-box	dipper
bucket	bowl	teapot
bushel	tumbler	jug
peck	jar	cup
firkin	mug	vase
pail	bottle	mortar
sieve	demijohn	
radish	$\frac{1}{2}$ pumpkin	walnut
beet	$\frac{1}{2}$ or $\frac{1}{4}$ apple	cocoanut
onion	$\frac{1}{2}$ orange	$\frac{1}{2}$ cocoanut
turnip	squash	many flowers
carrot	gourd	many leaves
pumpkin	acorn	
cuff	candle	cap
collar	roll of paper	lamp
hour glass	hat	muff
shawl strap		
spool	cage	duster
bell	mouse-trap	rolling-pin
wallet	lantern	pipe
round pond	tower	balloon
fountain	chimney	post

light-house cannon well
arch buoy pump
stump wigwam wasp's nest
log

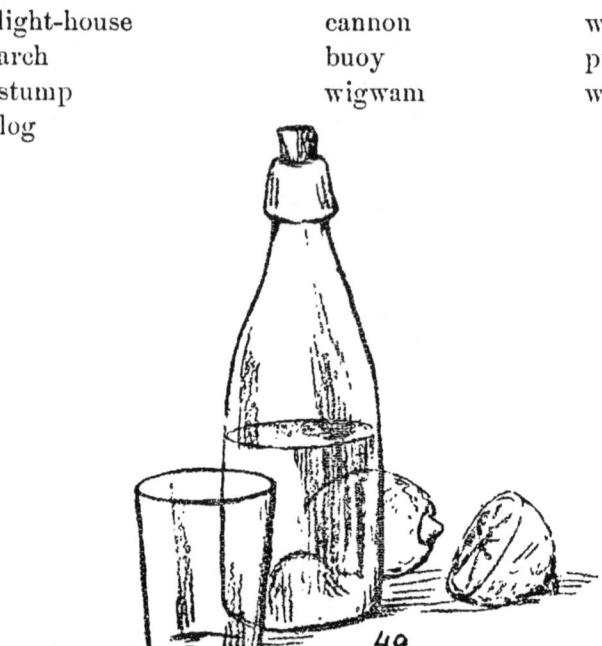

Few care to pay the price of success. One of the prices of success is to procure models. Place the following models before you and draw them.

The drawing, Fig. 49, is to suggest *how*, but is not intended to be used in place of models. Procure a real tumbler, a real bottle, and a real lemon.

27. Place a plain tumbler before you and draw it.
28. Draw the tumbler bottom up.
29. Draw the tumbler resting on its side.
30. Place a plain bottle before you and draw it.
31. Draw the bottle resting on its side.
32. Place one half of a lemon before you and draw it in three positions.

33. Place a plain bowl before you and draw it.
34. Place the bowl bottom up and draw it.

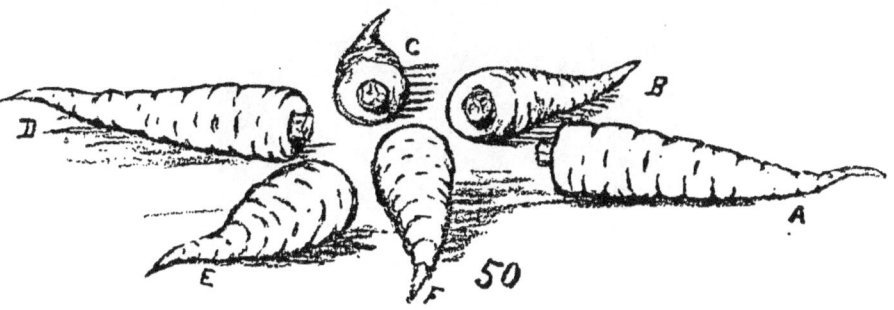

Procure for a model a carrot or radish. Do not use the drawings as models, but use them to suggest *how* the real model is drawn.

35. Place the carrot in the position of carrot A and draw it.
36. Draw the carrot in the position of B.
37. Draw the carrot in the position of C.
38. Draw the carrot in the position of D.
39. Draw the carrot in the position of E.
40. Draw the carrot in the position of F.

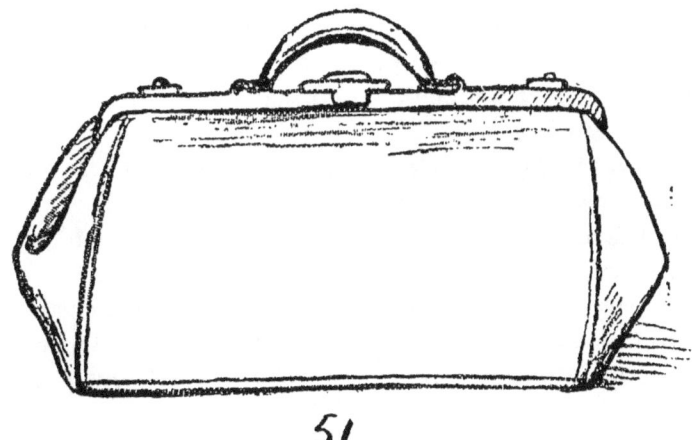

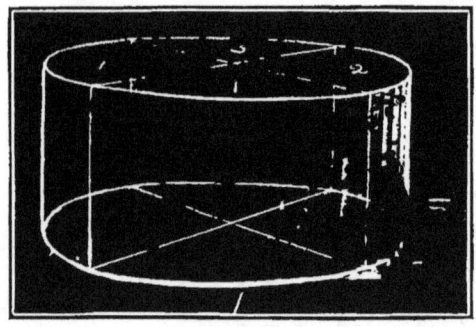

CHAPTER VIII.

Drill Exercises on the Cylinder.

To become proficient in anything requires much practice. To become proficient in drawing we must draw a great deal; we must draw from the object to acquire perceptive knowledge, and this, in order to be of practical use to us, must be turned into conceptive knowledge. Seeing gives ideas, which, to be of value, must in turn be used conceptively. In order to thoroughly understand the cylinder and similar forms, we must have drill work on the cylinder. *It is not enough to simply know, we must also be able to do.* The following work is to perfect our knowledge of the cylinder, and to so impress it on the mind that we may be able to use it whenever desired.

The doing improves the execution; the comparison with a model perfects the ideal.

Fig. 1 is a vertical cylinder drawn below the eye and divided into four equal parts by means of oblique horizontal receding lines, and each part numbered. Use for a model a potato or apple, cut in the form of a cylinder and divided into four equal parts, as in Fig. 1. *Use the model to perfect the idea.* Work out the following problems:

1. Draw Fig. 1 and remove parts 1 and 2.
2. Draw Fig. 1 and remove parts 1 and 3.
3. Draw Fig. 1 and remove parts 2 and 4.
4. Draw Fig. 1 and remove parts 1, 2 and 4.

When drawing a part it is often necessary to sketch the whole in order to draw the part correctly.

In the problems given below consider Fig. 1 as being hollow, like a round paper box.

5. Draw part 1 and remove the curved face. (The top, bottom, and side faces will remain.)
6. Draw parts 1 and 4 and remove the curved face.
7. Draw parts 2 and 3 and remove the front face.

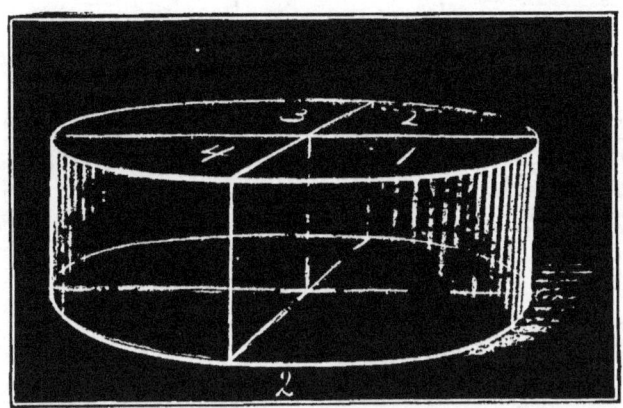

Fig. 2 is a vertical cylinder drawn below and at the left of the eye and divided into four equal parts by horizontal and horizontal receding lines.

Remove these parts as indicated in the following problems. *Do not use the center of vision.*

8. Draw Fig. 2 and remove part 1.
9. Remove part 1 and place it on 3.

10. Remove parts 2 and 4.
11. Remove parts 1 and 2 to below and at the right of the eye.
12. Separate all the blocks about a half inch.
13. Remove parts 1, 2 and 4.
14. Remove the upper half of block 1.
15. Remove the lower half of block 4.

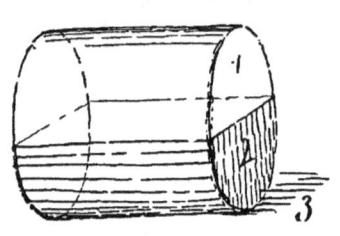 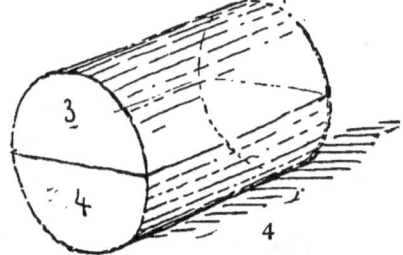

HORIZONTAL CYLINDER.

Fig. 3 is a horizontal cylinder drawn below and at the left of the eye, and Fig. 4 is an oblique horizontal receding cylinder drawn below the eye.

Depend on the unaided eye for the correctness of the drawing.

16. Draw Fig. 3 below and at the right of the eye.
17. Draw part 1 below and at the left of the eye.
18. Draw part 1 below the eye.
19. Draw part 2 below the eye.
20. Draw part 2 below and at the right of the eye.
21. Draw part 3 and remove the curved face.
22. Draw part 4 and remove the top face.
23. Slide part 3 to the right and away one-fourth its length.
24. Slide part 3 forward and to the left on part 4 one-fourth its length.

Fig. 5 is a horizontal receding cylinder, drawn below and at the left of the eye, and divided into two equal parts. Remove the

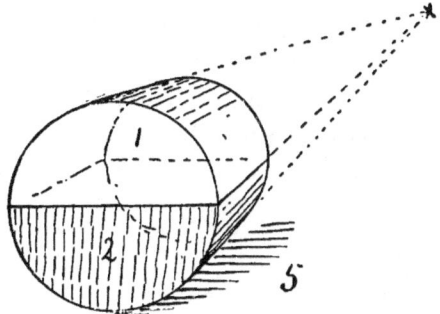

parts as indicated in the following exercises: *When the drawing is based on the horizontal receding cylinder, the center of vision may be used.*

25. Draw part 1 below and at the right of the eye.
26. Draw part 1 below and at the left of the eye. Remove the front face.
27. Draw part 1 below the eye.
28. Draw part 2 below the eye. Remove the top face.
29. Draw part 2 below and at the right of the eye. Remove the top face.

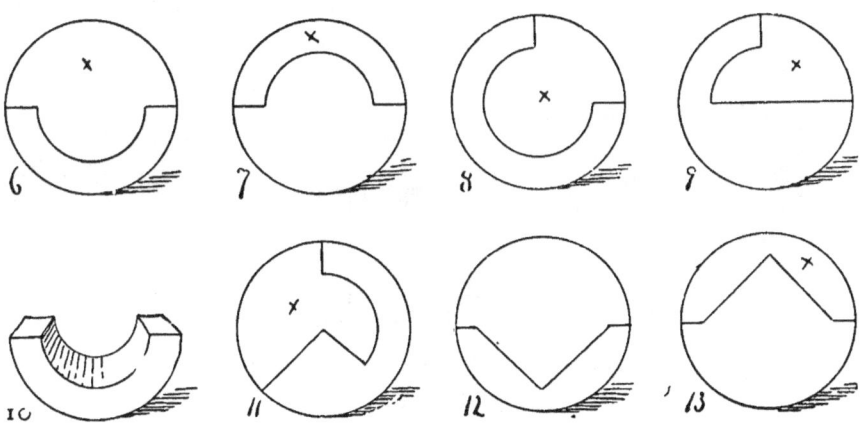

30. Draw part 2 below and at the left of the eye. Remove the curved face.

Figs. 6–13 represent the front face of cylinders drawn directly in front of the eye. On each face is marked a problem; the part marked X on each cylinder is to be removed as follows:

31. Draw Fig. 6 below the eye and remove the part marked X. (See Fig. 10.)

32. Draw Fig. 6 below and at the left of the eye and remove X.

33. Draw Fig. 7 below the eye and remove the part marked X. (See Fig. 14.)

34. Draw Fig. 7 below and at the right of the eye and remove the part marked X.

35. Draw Fig. 8 below and at the left of the eye and remove the part marked X.

36. Draw Fig. 9 below and at the left of the eye and remove the part marked X.

37. Draw Fig. 11 below and at the right of the eye and remove the part marked X.

38. Draw Fig. 12 below the eye and remove the part marked X to above the eye directly over the part marked Y.

39. Draw Fig. 13 below and at the right of the eye and remove the part marked X.

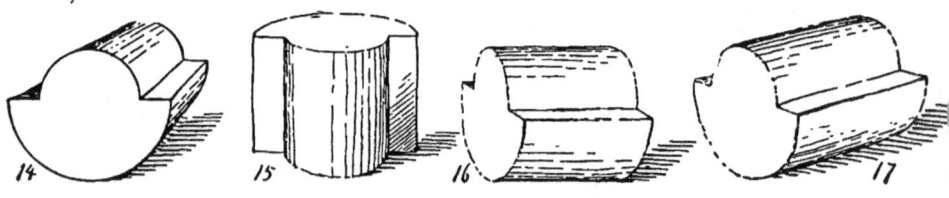

Fig. 14 represents Fig. 7 drawn below and at the left of the eye with X removed. Fig. 15 represents the same in a vertical position. Fig. 16 represents the same in a horizontal position, and Fig. 17 in an oblique horizontal receding position.

All of the figures, 6–13, may be drawn in any or all of these positions.

40. Draw Fig. 6 in the position of Fig. 16.
41. Draw Fig. 8 in the position of Fig. 16.
42. Draw Fig. 9 in the position of Fig. 17.
43. Draw Fig. 11 in the position of Fig. 17 receding to the left and away.

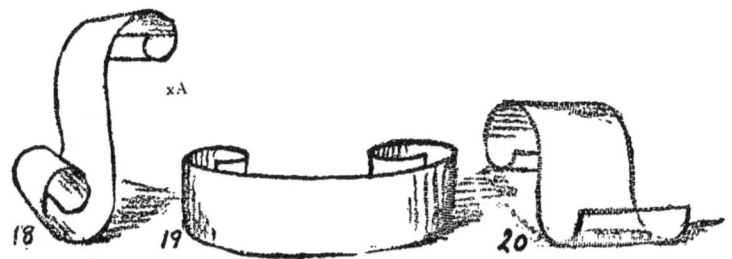

In drill work it is better to draw one object seven times than seven objects one time.

Use for a model a strip of paper about one inch wide, rolled around a lead pencil, as shown by models 18, 19 and 20.

Fig. 18 is drawn on the principle of a receding cylinder, Fig. 19 of a vertical cylinder, and Fig. 20 of a horizontal cylinder.

44. Draw scroll 18 as a horizontal cylinder at the left of the eye.
45. Draw scroll 18 as a vertical cylinder below the eye.
46. Draw scroll 18 with the center of vision at A.
47. Draw scroll 19 as a horizontal cylinder.
48. Draw scroll 19 as a receding cylinder below the eye.
49. Draw scroll 19 in the position of Fig. 17.
50. Draw scroll 20 as a receding cylinder.
51. Draw scroll 20 at the left of the eye.

We study the cylinder in certain set positions, easy to understand, easy to represent, and mechanical in construction, with the intention of absorbing the principle to the extent that the learner can use it universally so as to compass all positions, all conditions, from the drawing of an apple-stem to the great round world.

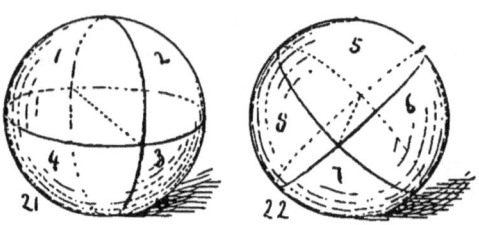

Figs. 21 and 22 are two spheres, each divided into four equal parts. Use for a model an apple with *one* quarter removed.

52. Remove part 1.
53. Remove part 2.
54. Remove parts 1 and 2.
55. Remove parts 3 and 4.
56. Draw part 1.
57. Draw part 1 below and at the left of the eye.
58. Draw part 2.
59. Place a half apple in the position of parts 3 and 4, and draw it.
60. Remove part 5.
61. Draw part 7.
62. Draw parts 6 and 8.

Fig. 23 is a cone drawn above the level of the eye and resting on the end of a stick or post.

For a model cut a semicircular disk from a piece of drawing paper, as represented by Fig. 24. Crease the center A for the apex of the cone and roll the base around and pin, as in Fig. 23.

AUGSBURG'S DRAWING. 115

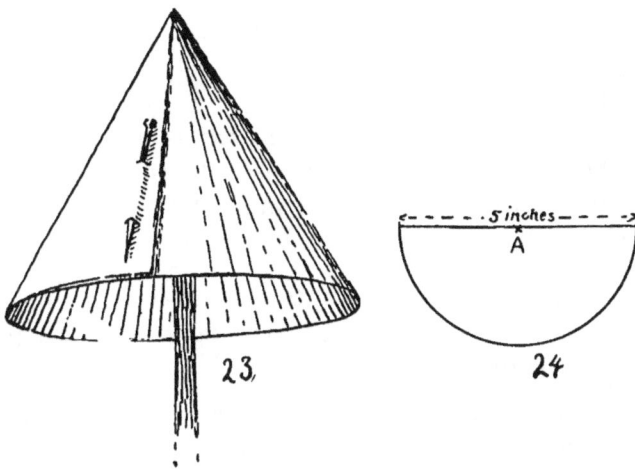

The paper may be less or more than a semicircle, according to the shape of the cone.

63. Draw a cone above the eye. (Fig. 23.)
64. Draw a cone below the eye.
65. Draw a cone below the eye, with the apex pointing downward.
66. Draw the cone resting on its side so that the inside can be seen.

67. Draw the cone resting on its side so that the inside cannot be seen.
68. Draw Fig. 25.
69. Draw a row of four wigwams, extending away.
70. Draw six wigwams at various distances away.
71. Draw a row of eight wigwams extending from the right away toward the horizon line.

Figs. 26, 27 and 28 represent three bird-houses drawn above the level of the eye and each representing one of the principle positions of the cylinder.

72. Draw Fig. 26 above and at the right of the eye.
73. Draw Fig. 26 below and at the left of the eye.
74. Draw Fig. 27 below the eye.
75. Draw Fig. 28.

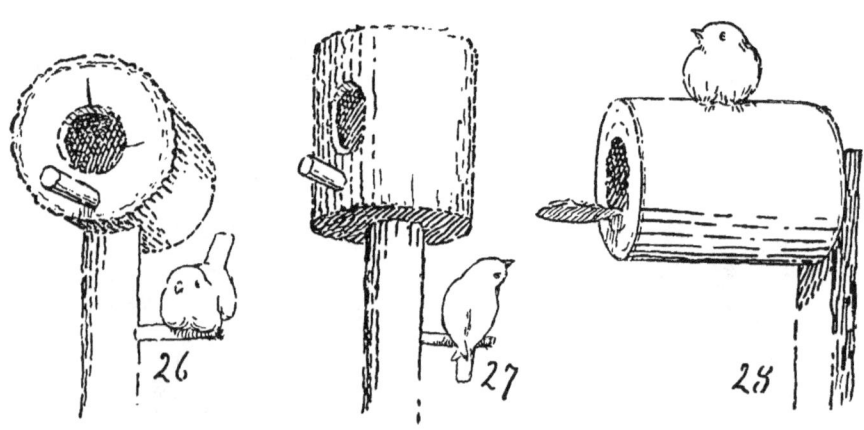

CHAPTER IX.

OBJECT DRAWING.

The Function of the Object.— It is the function of the object or model to stimulate to effort, to correct and elevate the ideal. The object or model is the perfecting element in growth. We all have stored away in the mind our ideal of a horse which is as perfect as our past experience, study and knowledge of the horse have made it. We wish to perfect this ideal. We can do so only by studying the horse—the model—still more closely. The artist turns to the model to perfect his thought. A noted landscape painter whose pictures are celebrated for their truthfulness to nature once said, "I never painted a picture from nature; I study from nature, but when I paint a picture, I am alone with my ideals." It is doubtful if any truly great picture was ever painted directly from nature.

Cannot Exactly Imitate the Object.— We cannot represent the object exactly as it appears to the eye. Imitate as closely as we will, we will find our best efforts are merely relative; nature is so superior that at our best we can only select, suggest, and interpret; and this is and should be our aim. We must *represent*, not *imitate*, must represent our own thought, our idea of the object we are drawing. Place a bird's nest before you. You can not *represent* it exactly as it appears to the eye, but you can *translate it* and the translation will not depend on your hand and eye, but on the perfection of your mental image — your concept, your thought, your idea of the nest. The object itself is not so important as your idea of the object. The idea is always first. *Your idea* of the bird's nest is what you draw, not the bird's idea, not somebody's else idea, but yours. The real nest is the model which stimulates and perfects *your* idea.

The Idea and Its Reproduction.— The idea, then, is first, and next to this idea is the mode of conveying it,—the technique, —the method. The idea is *the what*, the technique *the how*. There is nothing in the object to show you how to draw it; we learn this through the work of others; it is the legacy left to us by past experience. It is the accumulated knowledge of the world. "Method does not exist for its own sake but for better self-expression." Technique grows out of this expression. If we were left to ourselves to invent or discover a technique of our own, our efforts would be as crude as that of the savage.

Objects Not Suitable for Drawing.— Very few objects are suitable to learn to draw from. Those that are not suitable are: (1) Decorated objects; (2) delicately formed and finished objects; (3) complicated objects.

The decorations on an object tend to draw the attention from the form and to confuse the mind of the pupil. Finely formed and finished objects have required a high degree of skill to construct them, and require much the same skill to reproduce them in drawing; and complicated objects are confusing and difficult to understand.

Objects Suitable for Drawing.— In general, objects suitable for drawing are: (1) Plain and simple objects; (2) crudely-formed objects; (3) old, worn and broken objects; (4) natural objects.

Plain and simple objects are easy to understand, which is a strong factor in their successful reproduction. Crudely-formed objects have required little skill to fashion them and in consequence are easy to reproduce in drawing. Old, worn and broken objects are more interesting than new and whole objects. Much of their skilled accuracy is worn away, and the interesting element of use is seen to better advantage; besides, they are comparatively easy of reproduction.

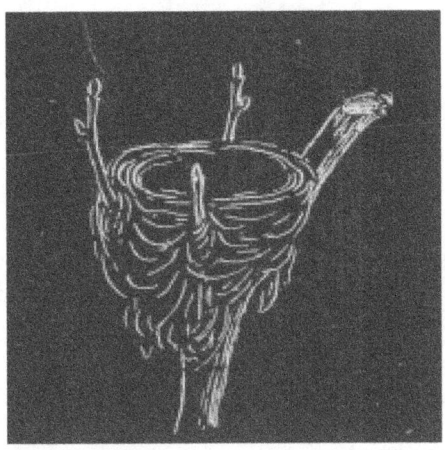

Natural objects are always interesting, but not always easy of reproduction. This comes from the fact that most natural objects must be translated. For example: The hat (Fig. 5) may be drawn almost line for line as it appears and all the details be represented, but in the bird's nest (Fig. 1) not one-tenth of the lines or details are reproduced, but just enough to suggest the leading features. When drawing natural objects it requires as much knowledge to know what to leave out as what to put in the drawing.

Size of Drawing.— The size of the drawing is usually adapted to the size of the paper on which the drawing is to be made. On the blackboard it should be of such a size as to show plainly across the room. A small object may be drawn larger than it is, just as a large object is usually drawn smaller. In general, the size of the object has nothing to do with the size of the drawing.

The following objects are suitable for drawing, if carefully selected:

Old, Worn, and Broken Objects.— Bowl, teapot, pitcher, jar, jug, scoop, sieve, oil-can, lamp, candle, flower-pot, bottle, pail, bucket, kettle, keg, barrel, cheese box, waste basket, grape basket, berry basket, market basket, umbrella, hat, cap, slipper, baby's shoe, rubber overshoe, hammer, saw, clamp, wrench, mallet, sickle, faucet, book, stool, valise, windwheel, grindstone, cannon, drum, toys, bag of grain, paper bag, roll of paper, dinner horn, flag, sled, wagon, cart, box-trap, mouse-trap, brooms, brushes, skates, stones, blocks of wood. Mounted birds, animals, and reptiles are also good objects to draw.

Small Objects Suitable to Hold in One Hand and to Draw with the Other.— Key, end of pencil, pen, clothes' peg, fish-hook, sinker, feather, wing, bird's tail, shears, scissors, top, knife, button-hook, pin, tack, nail, screw, pincers, corkscrew, pistol, needle, cup, mug, pipe, tooth brush, hair brush, padlock, book, swivel, three chain links, buckle, spool, ink, paste and mucilage bottles.

Natural Objects.— Box-elder seeds, ash seeds, milkweed pods, ears of corn; wheat, rye, barley and oat heads; acorns, horse chestnuts, oak galls, peppers, clusters of walnuts and peach stones; pumpkin, squash, cabbage, gourd, beet, tomato, onion, cucumber, turnip, potato, eggplant, carrot, apples, pears, quinces, peaches, grapes and plums; sweet peas, poppies, golden-rod, wax balls, rosebuds, roses, chrysanthemums, cosmos, asters and sunflowers; fir cones, pine cones, holly and mistletoe; birds' nests and wasps' nests; cocoanuts, bananas and lemons; leafless trees, such as poplar, box-elder, elm, ash, apple, cherry, willow, pear, plum and walnut; lilac buds, horse-chestnut buds, catkins, leaves, grasses and roots; flower buds, dandelions, pansies and violets; apple, peach and cherry blossoms; tulips, crocus, daffodil, radishes, cherries, strawberries, currants and gooseberries.

Bits of Landscape for Outdoor Drawing.— A stump, a log, a large stone, bunch of grass, a pile of rocks, a ledge of rock, a bluff, an island, point of land extending into the water, water trough, a wharf, corner of fence, gate, bars, stone wall, old mill, old tower, old bridge, any object that projects from the land into the water, an old tree, rock, haystack, ruins, bulrushes, dead tree, foot-bridge, path, road, spring, an old barn, shanty, shed, cabin or house, a boat, punt, scow or raft, a hammock, shock of corn or wheat.

When drawing bits of landscape, it is not necessary to draw more than you wish; therefore reject all you do not care to have appear in your drawing. For example: When drawing a stump, it is not necessary to draw the various objects about the stump simply because they are there; reject all you do not want.

How to Collect Objects.— If you ask your pupils to bring objects suitable for drawing, or ask them in a general way to bring a particular object, you invite failure. You must be specific. Suppose you have forty pupils and to-morrow you wish a lesson on maple leaves. Ask who will volunteer to bring fifty maple leaves for the lesson in drawing. From those who volunteer choose *one* and charge him with fifty maple leaves and hold him responsible, the same as if it were a debt of money. Write on the blackboard a list of the objects you desire and ask pupils to pick from the list an object they can bring. Charge each object to the pupil who agrees to bring it and hold him responsible.

A good collection of objects, a collection that the teacher has tried and knows thoroughly, is very valuable, far more so than new and untried objects, and is one of the most important elements of success in this work.

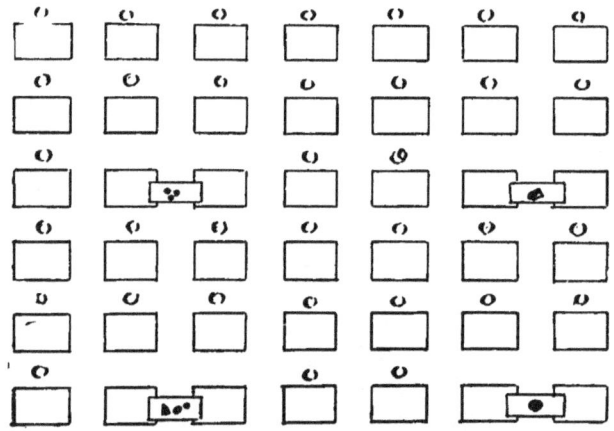

3

The Distribution of Objects.— With such objects as leaves, buds, twigs, nuts, some flowers and fruits, each pupil may be supplied with the same kind of object. With these small objects it is best the pupil be taught to hold the object in his left hand and to draw it with his right, as shown in Fig. 2. In this way the pupil will intuitively hold the model in both a good and easy position.

When the object is larger than can conveniently be held in the hand, then the models can be arranged on boards placed across the seats, as shown in Fig. 3. The boards may be made level by wedge-shaped cleats placed at the ends of the boards to neutralize the slant of the seats and make the board level.

Four boards are ordinarily enough if arranged judiciously. The pupils that sit in the seats across which the boards are placed, may draw at the blackboard or take vacant seats.

It is not necessary for all pupils to draw from the same object or the same kind of object.

Do not ask pupils to draw from a single object placed on the teacher's desk. Only a few will be able to see such an object sufficiently plain to make a good drawing from it.

Methods of Drawing Objects.— A method is an orderly way of doing. It is an aid to the judgment, but should in no way take the place of the judgment. The general method is the same as used in drawing the cylinder. It is adapted with simple modifications to the drawing of nearly all objects. The method is as follows:

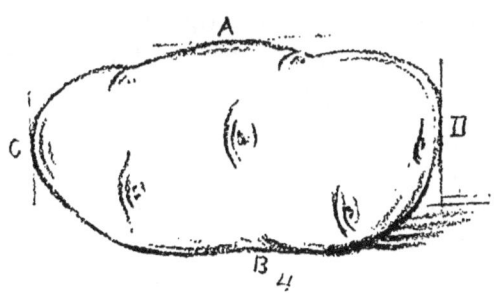

1. Take the height.
2. Find the length.
3. Find prominent points.
4. Block in, and finish.

For example, we will suppose the object is a potato, Fig. 4. (1) Place the object as in Fig. 4. (2) Take the height A B the size you wish the drawing. (3) Find the length, C D, by comparing with your pencil the height A B on the object and compare it with the length, C D, and then make the same comparison in the drawing. (4) Locate the eyes. (5) Block in and finish the drawing.

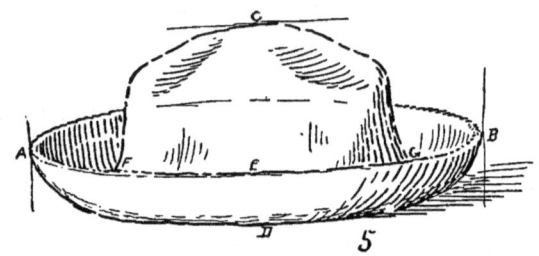

The hat, Fig. 5, is a little more complicated, but the method is the same.

1. Take the length A B.
2. Find the height C D.
3. Find prominent points, such as the width of the rim D E, and the width of the crown F G. Any point can be judged very accurately if the mind is concentrated on that point. We fail when we try to locate a point and draw at the same time.
4. Block in and finish the hat.

If the object is symmetrical and slender, like the scissors, Fig. 7, then —

1. Draw a median line as A B, Fig. 6.
2. Take the length A B.
3. With the unaided eye mark the point C, then D, then E.

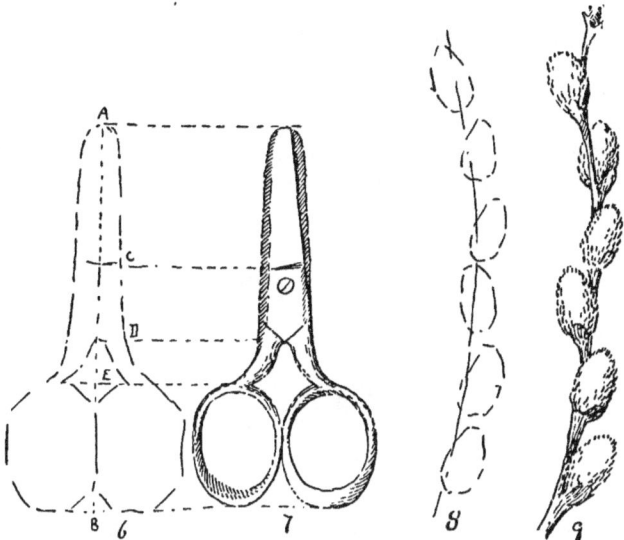

4. Roughly mark in the proportion.
5. Finish.

Fig. 8 shows the method of marking in slender unsymmetrical objects. First indicate the stem by a single light line, then the parts, and lastly finish as in Fig. 9.

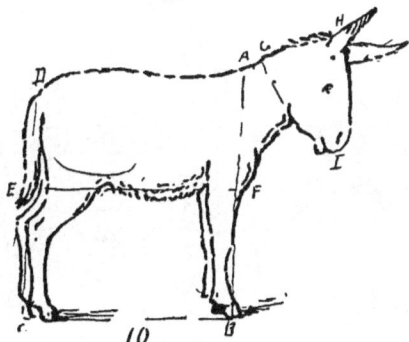

The recognition of the shape of the whole or part of the object is of great aid in marking in the general proportions. For example: recognizing in the donkey that the body, legs, and body and legs together are rectangular in shape and that the head is triangular, is a great aid in representing the general proportion. Familiar forms, such as triangles, rectangles, circles, ovals and ellipses are very common in the forms of objects, and when recognized, greatly aid in their reproduction.

Draw the Large Part First.— When an object, like a bird, consists of several parts, it is best to draw the large part first. When drawing birds, it is best to draw the body first, and to this add the smaller parts, such as the head, tail and feet. In most

objects it is easier to add the small parts to the large than to add the large parts to the small.

For the study and drawing of small animals, birds and reptiles, a common crayon box, with a piece of glass cut the size of the cover and made to slide in its place, is excellent. Holes should be bored into two sides to give plenty of fresh air. Mice, frogs, toads, salamanders, butterflies, beetles, spiders, etc., may be put in the box and studied and drawn in the school-room.

What to Represent.— Every student has the power of rejection in his drawings, but how to use this power to the best advantage must be taught. We cannot draw everything. We must discriminate between the very few essentials and the many non-essentials. One of the best means of deciding what to put in the drawing is to ask the question, What am I drawing? The bars, Fig. 14. Is it necessary then to put in the rocks and bushes, the trees and the distant hills beyond? No, *not unless you want them in*. You may draw the bars and that which relates to the bars, and leave out all the rest, unless you have a desire to put them in your drawing. It is your thought, your desire, your idea of the bars that you are to represent.

Grouping.— The main object in Grouping is *to please*. Grouping is placing objects in a pleasing relationship. There are laws and rules without end governing this relationship, but they

may be summed up in, *Does it please you? The arranging of objects in a pleasing group is based on the judgment, on your judgment, not mine, not Mr. Ruskin's, not anybody's else, but your own.* By using your own judgment, you will grow; by using the judgment of others, you lose your independence. Get all you can, from whatever source you can, but first make it your own before using it. If through the superior judgment of another your arrangement is shown to be faulty, learn all you can from the criticism, but still use your own judgment, your own powers of discrimination; look, think, compare, judge, and yet be receptive.

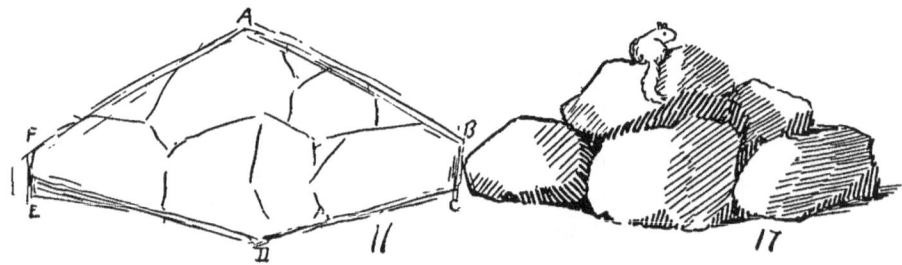

The most masterly way of drawing a group is to look at it as a unit, as one object, working from the whole to the part instead of from the part to the whole.

The process is very simple and is as follows:

1. Look at the group as a whole and note the shape of the figure that will enclose it, as Fig. 16.

2. With light lines "block in" this space, comparing the direction and position of each point with one another, until the proportions are marked in. "Feel" your way along. Look for the direction of the long lines, such as lines AB, CD, DE, and FA, Fig. 16.

3. Finish as in Fig. 17.

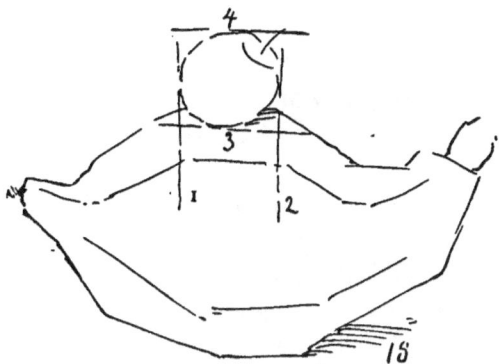

The relative size and position of two or more objects in a group may be gotten as follows:

1. Arrange the objects, say as in Fig. 18.

2. Draw the large object — in this case the squash.

3. To find the position and size of the apple, pass the pencil through the left edge of the apple and note where it crosses the squash. Mark this point on the squash as at 1, and from it draw a light vertical line. This will mark the left edge of the apple.

4. Find the right edge in the same manner and draw another vertical line, as at 2.

5. Pass the pencil through the lower edge of the apple and note where it crosses the squash. Mark this point as at 3 and draw a light horizontal line.

6. Draw line 4 with the unaided eye. The inclosed space will give the size and position of the apple.

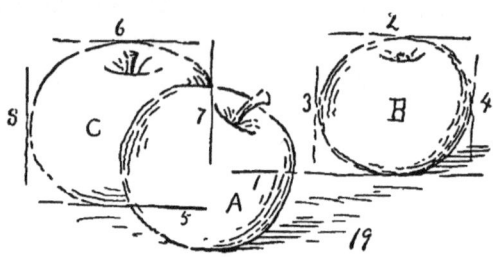

Measuring is simply an aid to the judgment and must not usurp its place. Measuring should decrease, but the judgment should increase.

1. Arrange objects similar to Fig. 19.
2. Draw the nearest object, *i. e.*, apple A.
3. To find the size and position of apple B, pass the pencil through the lower edge of apple B and note where the pencil crosses apple A. Mark this point in the drawing on apple A, as at 1, and from it draw a light horizontal line. Apple B will rest somewhere on this line.
4. To find the upper edge of apple B pass the pencil horizontally through the upper edge of apple B, and note how high the pencil is above apple A. Mark this point in the drawing as at 2 and draw a horizontal line. The top of apple B will be somewhere in this line.
5. Choose the point 3 with the unaided eye and draw a vertical line. Point 4 may also be located with the unaided eye.

6. Draw apple B.
7. In the same manner locate points 5, 6, 7, and 8 and draw apple C.

In all of the above work it will be seen that the principle is one of limitation, finding how far down, how far up, how far to the right, and how far to the left, an object extends compared with another object already drawn.

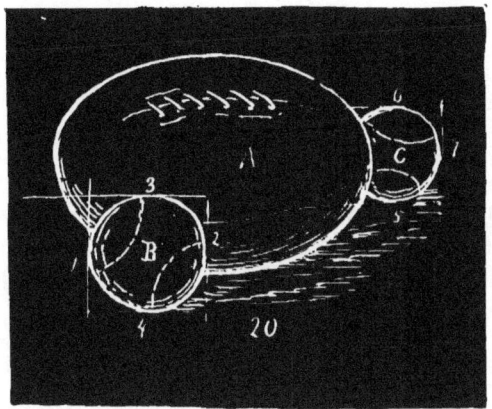

When one of the objects is larger and more prominent than the others, as in Fig. 20, draw the large object first.
1. Arrange objects similar to Fig. 20.
2. Draw the large object, as the football A.
3. The light lines show where to hold the pencil to find the points of limitation. Find points 1, 2, 3, 4, 5, 6 and 7, and there will be little trouble to mark in the proportion of balls B and C.

In Fig. 21 is combined both these methods of looking at the group as a whole and in detail. In such drawings both methods may be used to advantage. A, B, C, D is the general shape of the whole group which is broken up into the three forms.

Many good draughtsmen work from a point or center. For

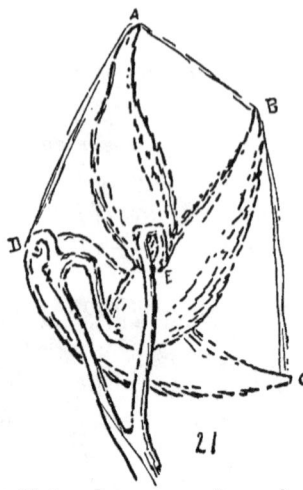

example, a point like E is chosen and each distance is estimated and each line drawn with regard to this point. This method is the direct opposite of looking at the group as a unit or whole.

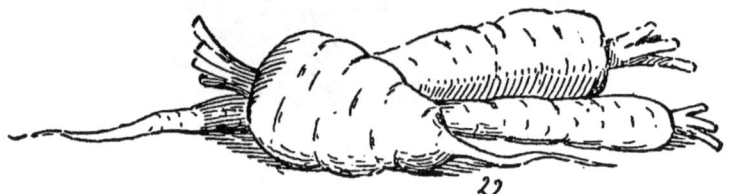

Pleasing groups are usually based on a geometrical form— the triangle, diamond, rectangle, pentagon, oval or ellipse. Some of the most pleasing groups are triangular in shape.

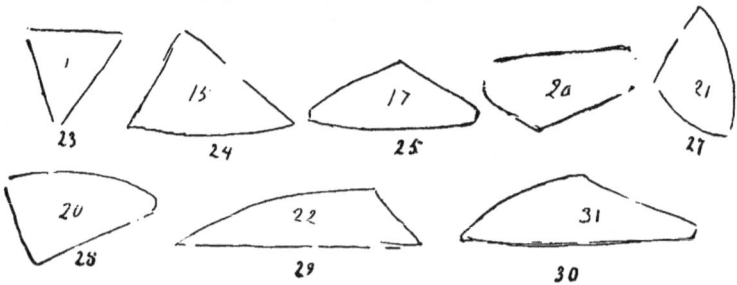

Figs. 23–30 represent the shape of the groups in this chapter; the inclosed number represents the number of the illustration. For example, Fig. 23 represents the shape of the bird's nest and its accessories, Fig. 1. Fig. 24 represents the shape of the barn and group of trees, Fig. 15.

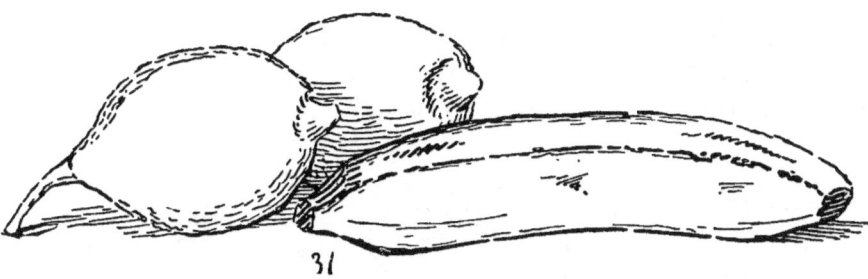

Line Accent.— Accent in drawing is very much like accent in talking, and both are caused by the same force — *thought*. Thought causes the modulation of the voice in talking and thought should cause the modulation of the line in drawing. It is not interesting to talk in a monotone, and it is as uninteresting to draw with only one kind of a line — a monoline.

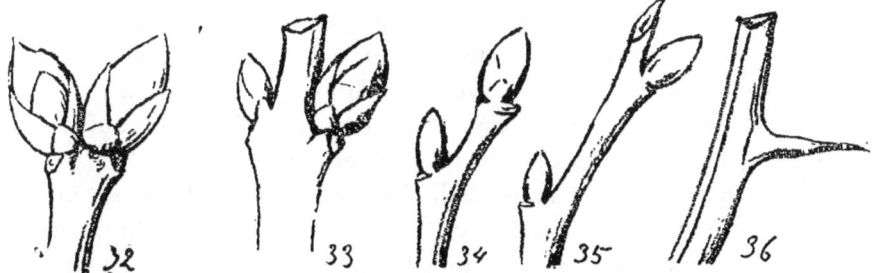

There are two conventional rules that govern line accent, both of which to some extent are observable in nature. They are:
1. Accent the nearest lines.
2. Accent the right hand and under lines.

But a higher and better way is to *accent the line in such a manner as to bring out your own thought.*

Accent your lines in drawing as you modulate your voice when talking. Begin by accenting some line, or some point simply because you want to. You may not place the emphasis in the best place, but if you are true to your thought, true to your wants, *your* best place will be found sooner, than to accent by rule or the wants of others. Observe the accent in the buds, Figs. 32-36, and in the calla lilies, Figs. 37 and 39.

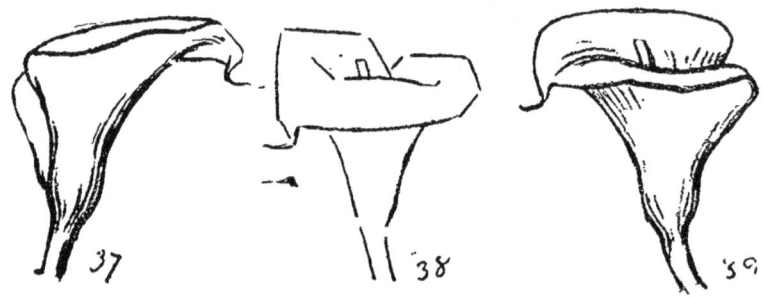

Concentration.— It is better to draw one object seven times than seven objects one time. Quality is more than quantity. Success and not variety is the key to the interest of children. They love to do that which they can do with some measure of success rather than take up new lines of work. They do not tire of one object as long as they feel a gain in power.

In general, much more will be gained by choosing one object that contains a variety of lines, like the calla lily, and drawing it every day until interest begins to wane. Choose a class of objects, such as keys, pocket knives, or shells, and draw them many times in different positions. Return to these objects whenever you wish to explain a new point, or to improve the execution.

Simplifying Objects.— Care should be taken when drawing natural objects, such as buds, leaves and flowers, to reduce the objects to their simplest form. If buds are drawn, only one, two or three should be on a stem, as in Figs. 32–36. One leaf with its stem and a small part of the stalk is enough for first efforts; and in flowers, one blossom alone is enough.

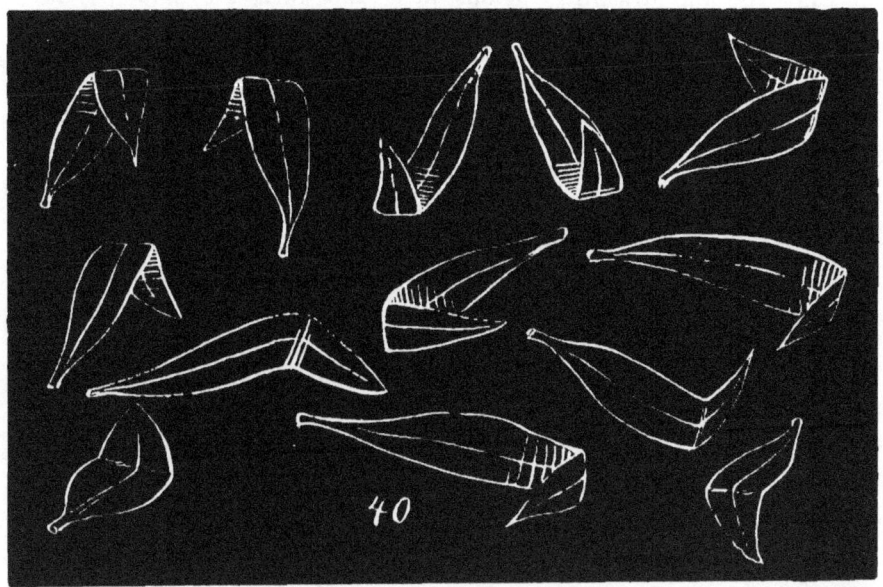

Suggestions for Teachers.— *These exercises are to suggest lines of work that may be overlooked by the busy teacher. The suggestions are grouped under the months of the year.*

August and September.— Encourage pupils to collect in a blank book drawings of bud, leaf, blossom and fruit of a tree.

Require several pupils to memorize the drawing of as many different leaves, and to reproduce them at a convenient time before the whole class.

Divide the study of leaves into (1) the single leaf. (2) The bending of a single leaf. (3) Two or three leaves grouped on a single stem.

Use at first short leaves with smooth edges similar to the lilac. Use a long, slender leaf, similar to the willow, to teach the bending of leaves. Make a sharp, artificial bend in the leaf, as shown in Fig. 40, and draw in various positions until the principle is learned, and then study the natural bends.

Leaves with a complicated outline, such as the maple, should not be used for first efforts.

The heads of wheat, rye, oats, barley and rice are beautiful models, also bols of cotton and ears of corn.

Encourage pupils to memorize the drawing of objects and then to reproduce them on the blackboard at any convenient time, such as the morning exercises or a Friday afternoon entertainment. From one to six pupils may make their drawings at the same time. All should be required to finish their drawings in one minute. It is better if the drawing can be accompanied by low music. For example, six pupils memorize the drawing of a leaf from as many different trees. They study and draw their leaf until they can reproduce it quickly and accurately from memory. At the proper time they all go to the blackboard together and each reproduces the leaf he has learned.

The vegetable family is the source of many good models. Among the best are the potato, carrot, turnip, tomato, and the various squashes.

October. — Use seeds and seed pods. The maple and box elder seeds are especially good, and the milk-weed pod, with its crooked stem, Fig. 21, is all that could be desired. The thistle, dandelion and the roadside seeds generally are interesting.

Nuts form an excellent group for the drawing class. A

cluster of hickory, hazel, butternuts or walnuts hanging to a small limb make very pleasing drawing lessons. The pecan, almond and acorn are also good. Peanuts may be made interesting by forming them into little men by adding arms and legs to them.

This is the month to find the various kinds of birds' nests. The old nests can be obtained at this time of year without wronging their former owners. The natural environment of the nest should be preserved as much as possible.

Have the pupils procure blank books and in them make a collection of the drawings of seeds and nuts.

The fruit family is the source of many fine models. The apple and similar fruits may be drawn whole, cut in halves and quarters, formed in groups, or attached to their native limb.

November.— Draw a pumpkin whole, cut in halves, quarters, and made into a jack-o'-lantern.

This is the time to study the turkey. Many of the feathers of the turkey make very good models for the drawing class.

Save wish-bones, and from them have a drawing lesson.

Hang up a broom, axe, saw, hatchet, gun, or sword where all can see it plainly and have it drawn.

Study the falling leaves.

December.—The holly and mistletoe, with their berries, may be studied and then used in Christmas decorations and designs.

A Christmas tree is a good feature for the drawing class. A small one about five years old is about right.

Hang several stockings up in the school-room for models to use in Christmas pictures.

Japanese lanterns hung about the room are cheerful and suggestive. They may be drawn singly or in groups.

Toys may be a feature of the drawing class.

January. — Skates, sleds, muffs, and mittens will make good models for several lessons in drawing.

A caged rabbit is an excellent model.

Shells contain many elements that make them ideal as models.

Keys occupy little space and are excellent to hold in one hand and draw with the other.

Children seldom tire of drawing pocket knives. Old and broken ones are preferable.

A good collection of objects is one of the main elements of success in the drawing class. A collection that the teacher has tried, proven and learned is invaluable. Such a collection is a growth and cannot be procured at once. Simple *possession* does not make a model one's own. We make it our own through use.

Place small objects along the blackboard rail for pupils to draw at such times as they are at liberty from other tasks.

February. — Study the leafless trees. Find examples of vertical branching, horizontal branching and irregular branching. It is not necessary or desirable to represent all the branches of the tree when drawing it. Aim to show character rather than quantity.

Mounted birds and animals form a fine line of models. A very effective way of utilizing a single specimen is to place it in a favorable position before a vacant seat and make the drawing of it a special feature for honorable merit.

Have the pupils collect in a blank book drawings of the various hats and caps. Begin with the cloak-room and extend to the museum, and lastly to pictures.

Many vases and pitchers have fine outlines. They should, however, be free from decoration and simple in form.

A small rubber plant, Chinese lily and calla lily may be made the source of many drawing lessons.

March.— Watch for the pussy willows, and take advantage of them when they come.

The robin, bluebird and blackbird can be made much of if a mounted specimen of each can be procured.

If a tree can be plainly seen from the window, have a cosy place prepared where it can be drawn under favorable conditions and when convenient let one or more pupils draw it. In this way the changes from the bare limbs to full foliage can be studied.

Chicks and ducklings may be placed in a small cage and used as objects for many interesting lessons.

April.—The buds as they come out in the spring are interesting. The lilac, horsechestnut, poplar, box elder, willow and the various catkins are among the best.

Arbor day should be made a great day in drawing. Have six pupils each memorize a tree and reproduce it at the Friday afternoon exercises.

Let three pupils each represent a leafless tree. One of vertical branching, like the poplar, one of horizontal branching, like the beech or spruce, and one of irregular branching, like the maple.

At Easter time make a study of eggs. Arrange eggs in a nest and draw them. Broken shells are good models.

An aquarium may be made the source of much interest. Tadpoles, fishes and many water bugs may be studied and then used in the drawing class.

Combine nature study and drawing whenever practicable.

May.—Take advantage of the wild flowers as they are brought to the school-room.

Have pupils use blank books in keeping watch of the development of a bud by drawing it at regular intervals.

Have the pupils make a collection of the different buds as they come out, by drawing them in a blank book.

June.— Find some picturesque house, barn, water-trough, tree, old mill, or similar object in your vicinity, and send pupils there to draw it and then reproduce it on the blackboard.

Berries make very good models if picked with a stem and a few leaves.

Have pupils draw a tree as it appears silhouetted against the sky.

A large rock, a point of rocks, a group of large and small boulders form a fine line of work.

A boat is an excellent model for those living on a river, lake or coast. Have the different kinds of sailing vessels, such as a schooner, ship, brig, brigantine, bark, barkentine, drawn on the blackboard ; also the different kinds of steamboats.

When the circus comes to town, make it a source of profit to the drawing class by asking those who are going to attend to make drawings of the tent, wagons, etc., to reproduce on the blackboard.

CHAPTER X.

THE TRIANGULAR PRISM.

Perceptive and Conceptive Drawing.— There are two kinds of drawing — perceptive and conceptive. Perceptive is drawing what you see; conceptive is drawing what you think. Perceptive is object drawing; conceptive is thought drawing. Perceptive drawing is the basis of conceptive drawing. These two phases of drawing merge into each other at every point, so that a purely perceptive or conceptive drawing is not common.

To the teacher, conceptive drawing is more useful than perceptive. If she wants to use the drawing of a tree, a rock, or a squirrel, it is not practical for her to go in search of them. She must be able to draw them at once and at the time they are needed.

How to Draw Conceptively.— One can learn how to draw conceptively in the same manner that we learn to use words and numbers conceptively, in the same way we teach children to use numbers and words conceptively. We teach children the use of words perceptively and then lead them to use them in little stories — to use them conceptively. We teach them the use of numbers perceptively and then we lead them to use them conceptively. We can learn to use drawing conceptively in the same way. We learn the principle of drawing the box, the cylinder, and the prism perceptively, and then we use these principles conceptively. We learn a principle by studying the object, then in the drill exercise by degrees learn to use it conceptively. Object drawing alone will not train one to draw conceptively. The object is the material source of the image, but it does not train the mind how to use this image any more than a mere knowledge of words will enable one to write an essay. A fine penman is not necessarily a fine writer, nor a good draughtsman necessarily an artist. One of the most important aims in teaching is to turn perceptive knowledge into conceptive; to get the principle out of the arithmetic into the mind of the pupil, where he can use it conceptively; to learn perceptively the meaning of words and things so that the knowledge may be reproduced in thought form. We should have the same end in view in drawing. As soon as we have learned how to draw the triangular prism perceptively, we should use this knowledge conceptively. To do this, the following is a good method:

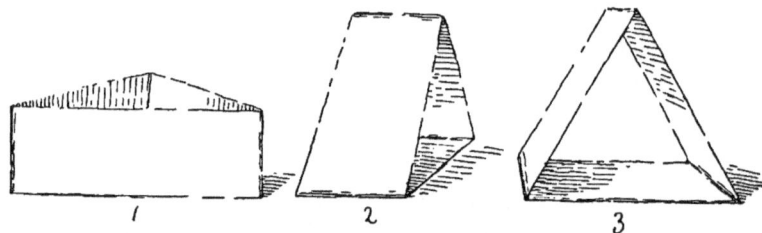

1   2   3

The Triangular Prism may be made the basis of objects containing oblique lines. For convenience its study is divided the same as the cylinder, into (1) the vertical triangular prism, Fig. 1; (2) the horizontal triangular prism, Fig. 2; (3) the horizontal receding triangular prism, Fig. 3.

Models.— Use for a model a strip of stiff paper 9x1½ inches, folded as in Fig. 4, with the lap glued, pinned, or a light elastic slipped around it.

Vertical Prism.— Place the prism before you as in Fig. 4, and observe: (1) That there are four sets of lines,— 1, 1, 1, 2,

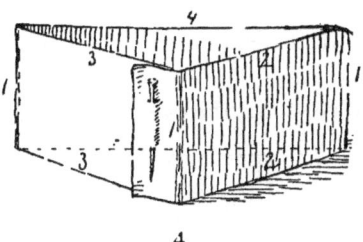

2, 3, 3, and 4, 4. (2) That the lines of each set are parallel, lines 2, 2, and 3, 3, being receding, converge slightly but they represent parallel lines, and are called parallel. They should converge in the drawing, but *they should not appear to converge.* They should appear natural.

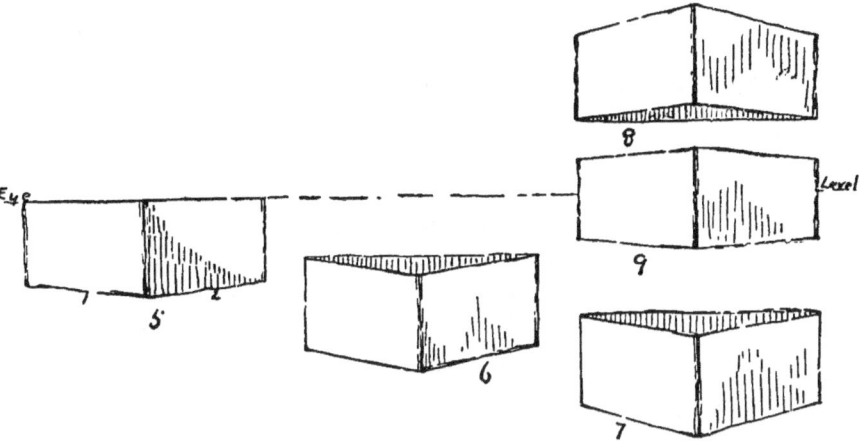

Hold the prism in the position of Fig. 5, then in the position of Fig. 6, Fig. 7, Fig. 8, and Fig. 9, and observe: (1) That when the top is on a level with the eye, it is a horizontal line. Fig. 5. (2) That when the top is below the level of the eye, it can be seen, and the farther it is below the eye, the wider it is drawn. Figs. 6 and 7. (3) That the bottom is drawn wider than the top in Figs. 5, 6, and 7 because it is farther below the eye. (4) That the bottom can be seen when drawn above the eye. Fig. 8. (5) That neither the top nor bottom can be seen when drawn on a level with the eye. Fig. 9.

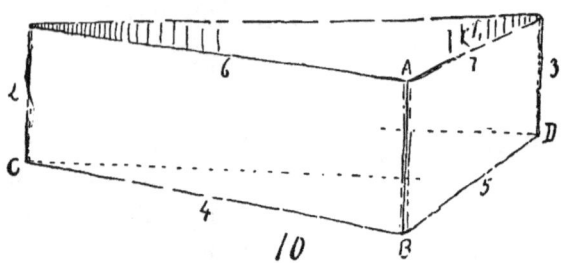

The vertical prism is drawn the same as the box. (See Exact Drawing, Chapter VI.) This is done in general, as follows:
1. Take the nearest vertical line.
2. Find the remaining vertical lines.
3. Find the corners.
4. Finish.

Stated more specifically, the process is as follows:
1. Place the object, say as in Fig. 10.
2. Take the nearest vertical line A B.
3. Find the remaining vertical lines 2 and 3.
4. Find the corners C and D and draw lines 4 and 5.
5. Draw lines 6 and 7 parallel with 4 and 5.
6. Finish.

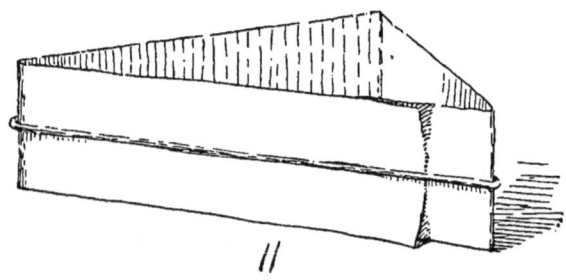

DRILL EXERCISES.

In the following exercises do not use the pictures, but a real prism for a model.
1. Place the prism in the position of Fig. 1 and draw it.
2. Place the prism in the position of Fig. 4 and draw it.
3. Place the prism in the position of Fig. 5 and draw it.
4. Place the prism in the position of Fig. 6 and draw it.

5. Place a book in the position of Fig. 12 and draw it.
6. Place a book in the position of Fig. 13 and draw it.
7. Place a book in the position of Fig. 14 and draw it.
8. Place a book in the position of Fig. 15 and draw it.
9. Place a book in the position of Fig. 16 and draw it.
10. Place a book in the position of Fig. 17 and draw it.

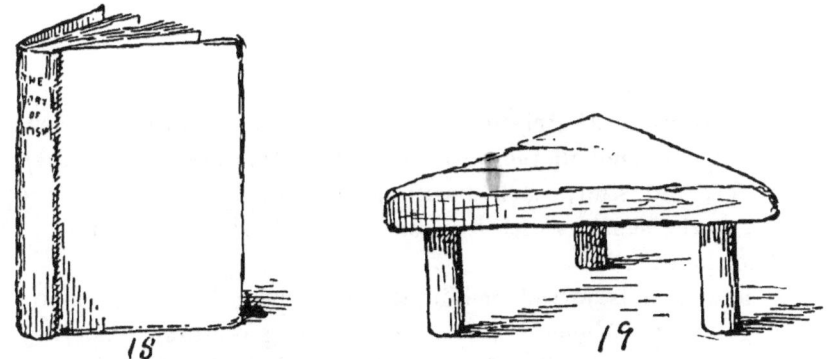

Draw the stool, Fig. 19, conceptively, that is, without a model, in the following positions:

11. Draw Fig. 19.
12. Draw Fig. 19 in the position of Fig. 4.
13. Draw Fig. 19 in the position of Fig. 5.
14. Draw Fig. 19 bottom side up.

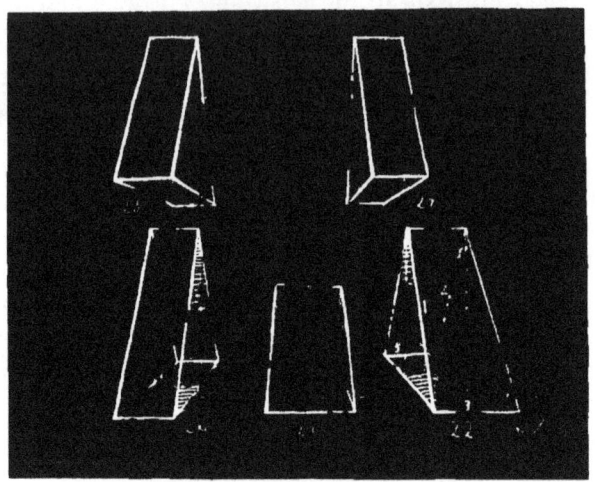

THE HORIZONTAL PRISM.

The Horizontal Prism.— Hold the paper model in the position of Fig. 20, then in the position of Fig. 21, then Fig. 22, then 23 and 24, and study each position closely. Observe that the principle is the same as with the box and the horizontal cylinder in regard to the eye.

A new line is introduced in these figures; Lines 1, 1, and 2, 2, Fig. 22 are *oblique receding lines*. Being receding lines they will converge slightly, line 5 being shorter than line 4, and line 4 shorter than line 3, because farther away.

Observe, also, that the apex is over the center of the base.

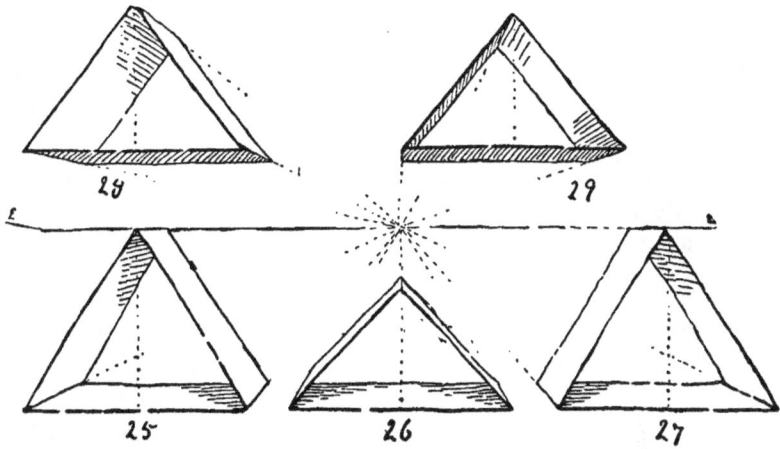

The Receding Prism.— Figs. 25-29 represent the various positions of the horizontal receding prisms. Hold a model in position and compare it with each drawing line for line. Observe each point both on the model and in the drawing. Aim to see and know the principle.

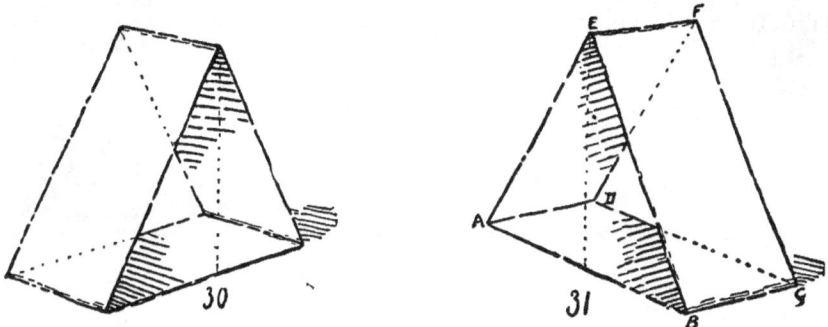

Figs. 30 and 31 are oblique horizontal receding prisms. Oblique, because at an angle with the picture plane; horizontal, because the principal lines are horizontal with the plane of the earth; receding, because the lines recede from you.

Drawing the Prism.— After the instruction given in the drawing of the cube and cylinder, it will be unnecessary to give specific directions in the drawing of the prism — a few general suggestions will be enough.

The following is a good plan for all positions of the prism.
1. Draw the base A B C D, Fig. 31.
2. Find the apex E and F.
3. Finish.

Objects similar to the triangular prism are comparatively few in number. They are limited largely to *objects used in parting*, such as a wedge and the roofs of houses.

Drill Work.— Drill work is as necessary in drawing as in numbers, language, and music, and without it the knowledge gained is very apt to be fugitive and soon forgotten. Drill is assimilating the knowledge so that it can be used in thought form. One of the chief ends of drill work should be to acquire the principle, so that it can be used as an aid in the expression of thought.

DRILL EXERCISES IN PERCEPTIVE DRAWING.

15. Place the model before you in the position of Fig. 20 and draw it.
16. Draw the model in the position of Fig. 22.
17. Draw the model in the position of Fig. 24.
18. Draw the model in the position of Fig. 25.
19. Draw the model in the position of Fig. 26.
20. Draw the model in the position of Fig. 27.
21. Draw the model in the position of Fig. 28.
22. Draw the model in the position of Fig. 29.
23. Draw the model in the position of Fig. 30.
24. Draw the model in the position of Fig. 31.

DRILL EXERCISES IN CONCEPTIVE DRAWING.

25. Draw prism 35 and remove X.
26. Draw prism 36 and remove X.
27. Draw prism 37 and remove X.
28. Draw prism 38 and remove X.

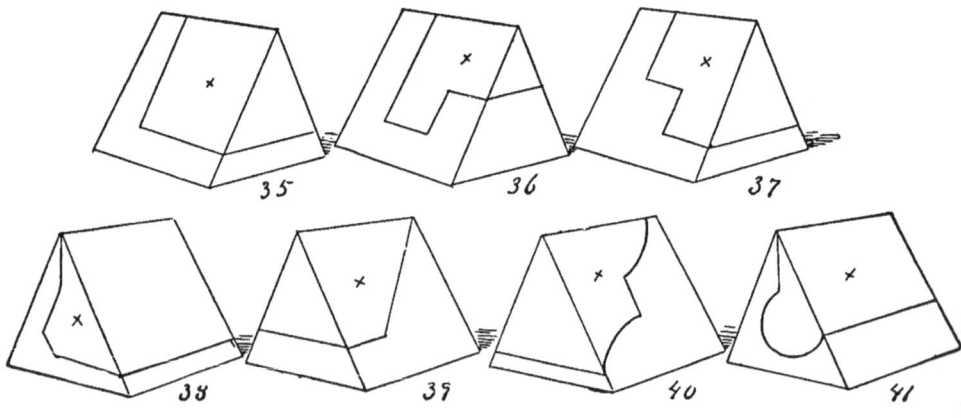

AUGSBURG'S DRAWING. 151

29. Draw prism 39 and remove X.
30. Draw prism 40 and remove X.
31. Draw prism 41 and remove X.

NOTE.— The problems represented by Figs. 25–30, Chapter III., and Figs. 6–13, Chapter VIII., may be cut from the triangular prism in any position.

32. Draw Fig. 32.
33. Draw Fig. 32 as a horizontal prism at the right of the eye.
34. Draw Fig. 33.
35. Draw Fig. 33 in the position of prism 35.
36. Draw Fig. 34.
37. Draw Fig. 34 in the position of prism 38.
38. Draw Fig. 42.
39. Draw Fig. 42 in the position of prism 38.

CHAPTER XI.

REFLECTIONS.

Use for a reflecting surface a piece of bright tin, 6x9 inches or longer. Do not use a mirror, as the mirror reflects from the under surface of the glass and leaves a space between the object and its reflection. Place the tin on the table before you, about two feet away, and about the length of a lead pencil below the eye.

Place on the tin a small block or box similar to Fig. 1 and observe:
 1. That the reflection is like the box, but inverted.
 2. That the reflection is the same size as the box.
 3. That the length of the edges A B, D E, and G H are the same length as their reflections, B C, E F, and H I.
 4. Observe that the receding lines of the reflection are parallel to and obey the same law as the receding lines of the box.

Make a model out of a strip of drawing paper, about 1x9 inches long, similar to Fig. 2. Place this model on the tin as in Fig. 2 and observe:
 1. That the vertical lines marked 1, 1, 1, 1, are continued in the reflection, and are of the same length.
 2. That the set of lines marked 2 in both object and reflection are parallel.

AUGSBURG'S DRAWING. 153

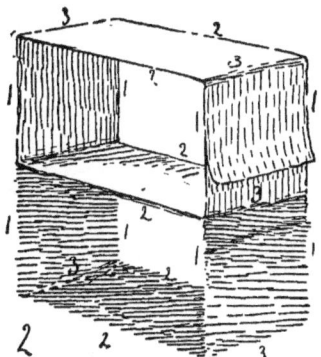

3. That the set of lines marked 3 in both object and reflection are parallel.

NOTE.—Of course it is understood that all parallel receding lines converge and if continued would come together at a point.

Place a small cylinder on the tin and observe:
In Fig. 3 that the longer axis is not vertical.
In Fig. 4 that the top of the cylinder can be seen, but that it does not show in the reflection.

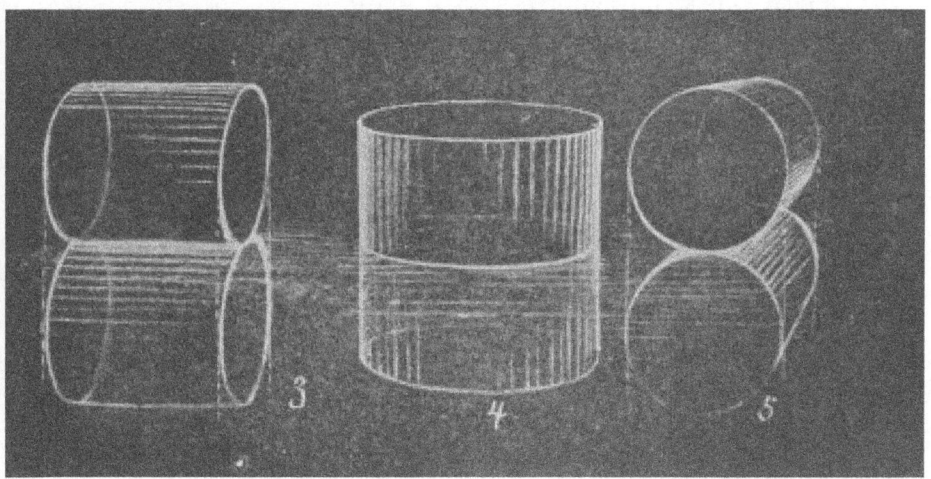

In all the cylinders that the reflection is not outside of a vertical line dropped from the outer edges of the cylinders.

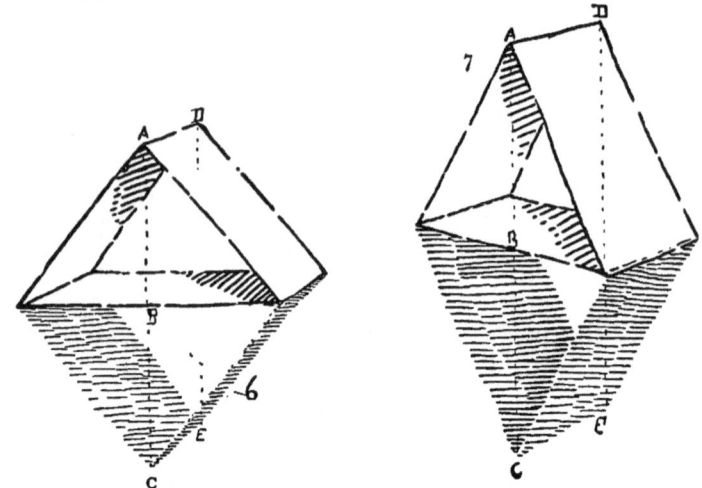

Construct a triangular prism out of a strip of drawing paper 1x7 inches and place it on the tin, and observe:

That A and C are in the same vertical line.

That C is as far below B as A is above it.

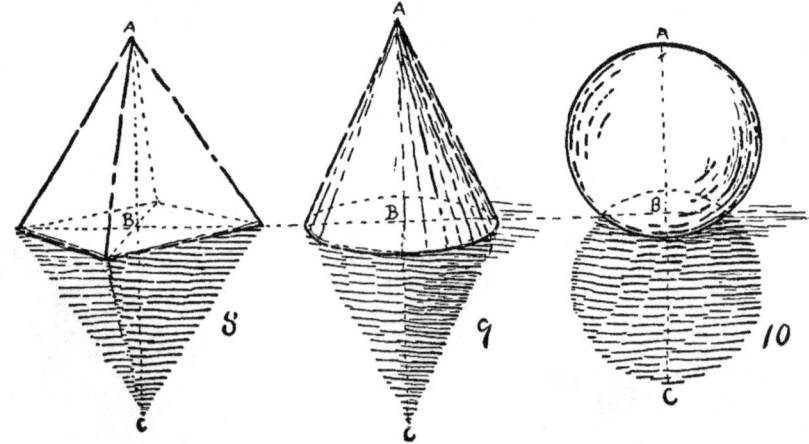

That E is directly under D and in the same vertical line.
Observe the above in both Figs. 6 and 7.

Place a pyramid, cone, and sphere on the tin and observe that A B in each is equal to B C, and that the point C is as far below

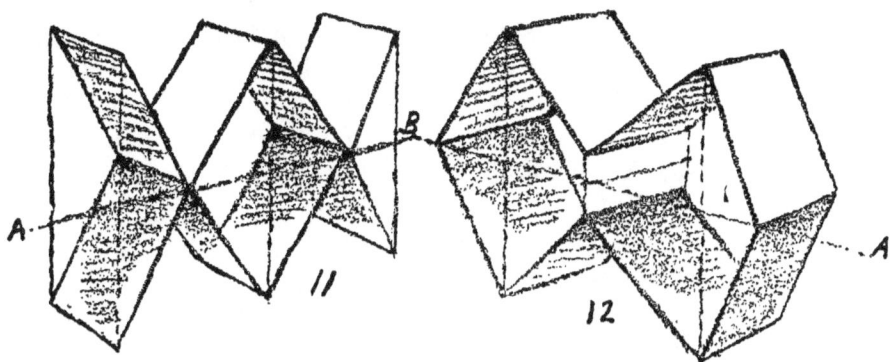

the point B as A is above it; that A and C are in the same vertical line.

Observe the above in Figs. 8, 9 and 10.

Figs. 11 and 12 are strips of paper doubled up in the form of a W and an M and placed on the tin. Place similar strips on the tin and observe:

1. That a line like A B passing through the points of contact with the surface of the tin marks that surface.

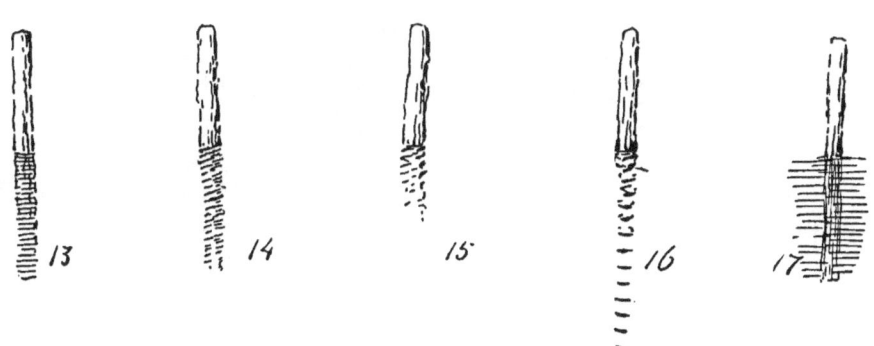

2. That each point of the paper is reflected as far below this line as the point is above it, and that the reflection and the point reflected are in the same vertical line.

Reflecting Surfaces.—All surfaces reflect light more or less, but only polished surfaces reflect images. In nature, water is the great reflector. This is perhaps the greatest characteristic of water. Perfectly still water is a mirror, and reflects images from its surface as accurately as a glass mirror. Reflections are as varied as the conditions under which they are seen. Figs. 13–17 illustrate several of these conditions.

Fig. 13 represents the reflection of perfectly still water.

Fig. 14 represents water slightly in motion.

Fig. 15 represents the water so much in motion that the reflection is only suggested.

Fig. 16 shows a reflection influenced by smooth ripples. Often this reflection is longer than the object reflected.

Fig. 17 shows the reflection of a hard, smooth, or polished surface, like that of ice.

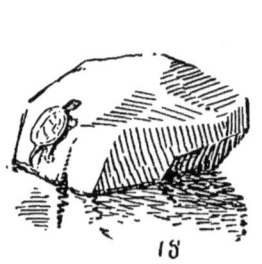
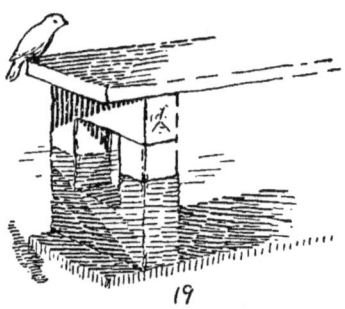

Observe in Fig. 18 that the reflection of the stone is only suggested and in Fig. 19 it is almost as plain as the object reflected. In water there are all kinds and conditions of reflections. They vary from a perfect mirror-like image, through all the changes made by current, wind and waves, to complete obliteration. In general, the reflection is darker than the image reflected. So multifarious are the conditions that modify and change reflections, that much liberty may be taken with them, the same as with light and shade. The reflection is subordinate to the idea that is

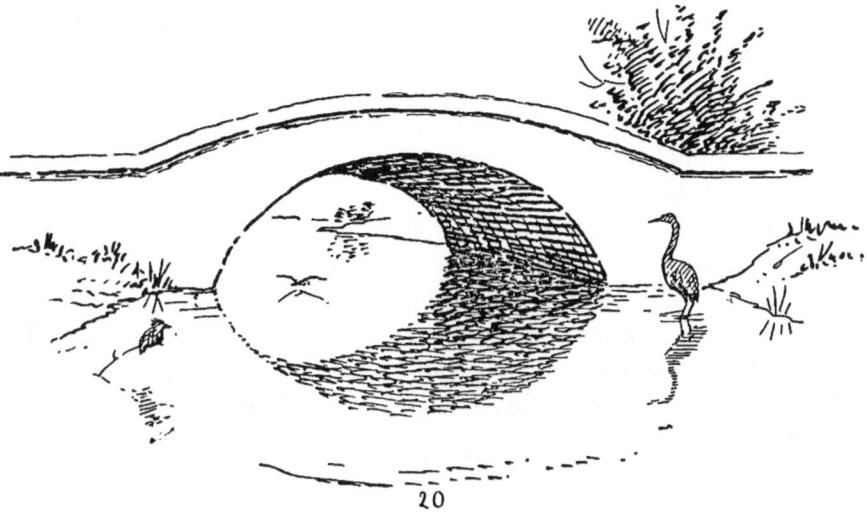

being represented and as such should not be allowed to make its own conditions, but is the servant of the mind. This is only so, however, after its laws and principles have been mastered.

One of the best places to study reflections is along the shore of a pond or stream. A rock, a stump, a log, a point of rocks, a bridge, bulrushes, an island, or a wharf, are all excellent objects to observe, study and represent; but before studying these objects it is necessary to study the principle of reflections thoroughly.

DRILL EXERCISES.

Place the following objects on the tin and draw them.

1. A small box.
2. Make a paper model of a box, triangular prism, a cone and a cylinder and place each on the tin in various positions and draw them until you thoroughly understand the principle.
3. Place an apple on the tin and draw it. A half apple. A quarter apple.
4. Fold a strip of paper similar to Fig. 11, and place it on the tin and draw it.
5. Draw the paper bottom up.
6. Draw the paper resting on its edge.
7. Place a small stone on the tin and draw it.
8. The following are excellent objects to draw that may be found along the shore of a stream, lake, or pond: Rock, stump, log, pier, boat-house, boat, bridge, point of rocks, fence, bushes, rushes, etc.

Drawing Helps

The following sets of cards are for aids in the teaching of certain phases of drawing. There are twenty-five cards in each set, each representing a drawing made in the simplest manner and illustrating in a uniform and progressive way

ACTION DRAWING
CHALK DRAWING
THE DRAWING OF TREES
THE DRAWING OF BOATS
THE DRAWING OF HOUSES

These cards are suitable for all grades. They are arranged in sets as follows:

ACTION DRAWING

Set I. The Action of Little Men
Set II. The Action of Deer
Set III. The Action of the Horse
Set IV. The Action of the Dog

DRAWING HELPS

Set I. Chalk Drawing
Set II. The Drawing of Trees
Set III. The Drawing of Boats
Set IV. The Drawing of Houses